GREATEST
HOLLYWOOD
SCANDALS

THE WORLD'S GREATEST HOLLYWOOD SCANDALS

JOHN MARRIOTT
AND
ROBIN CROSS

OCTOPUS BOOKS

Contents

Published in 1989 by Octopus Books Limited
Michelin House, 81 Fulham Road,
London SW3 6RB

First published in 1989
ISBN 0 7064 38914

Typeset by
Rowland Phototypesetting Limited
Bury St Edmunds, Suffolk
Printed in Great Britain by
The Bath Press Limited
Bath

Wallace Reid, the first Hollywood star to die from drug abuse.

As Cole Porter observed, some get their kicks from cocaine. In the 1920s this tart observation might have applied to half of Hollywood, where the white powder was a universal party-pepper and pick-me-up. Director Byron Haskin recalled that at one wild party a room was set aside for a huge cut-glass bowl brimming with cocaine and a pile of thoughtfully provided rolled-up papers.

Only a few years earlier cocaine had been a fit subject for sly humour. In 1916 Douglas Fairbanks had appeared in *The Mystery of the Leaping Fish* as a manic detective called 'Coke Ennyday'. That year Hollywood was visited by Aleister Crowley, the 'Wickedest Man in the World', who described the movie people as a bunch of 'cocaine-crazed sexual lunatics'. Clearly everyone was having a wonderful time in the homes and clubs of Hollywood.

The majority survived to tell the tale, reminiscing in their declining years about the wild excesses of the Jazz Age. But drugs claimed their victims, among them some of silent cinema's brightest stars.

Double Speed for Wally

Wallace Reid was the first, but by no means the last Hollywood big name to die a drug addict. It was medical negligence rather than hedonism which led to the death of one of Paramount's most bankable stars of the early 1920s. Nevertheless, the newspapers had a field day, cramming their inside pages with imaginative reconstructions of the padded cell in a mental home in which a half-crazed Reid gibbered his life away. The irony of his death was that the charming and athletic Reid had specialized in playing breezy all-American types. No one typified the clean-cut collar-ad go-getter better than Wally Reid.

Success trapped Reid on a treadmill of cheaply produced starring vehicles, which studio boss Jesse Lasky referred to as the 'frozen custard machine'. This hectic pace helped to kill him. It was while filming *The Valley of the Giants* (1919) on location in the High Sierra that Reid was given doses of morphine to relieve the pain of a back injury sustained in a train crash. The treatment continued in hospital, and when Reid emerged he had become addicted. For a while Wally managed to keep up appearances, but by the time he was cast as a boxer in *The World's Champ* (1922) his strength was fast ebbing away and he could hardly stand. For Paramount, Reid had quite literally become a wasting asset, and there were millions of dollars riding on his career. Fearing the worst, the studio insisted that a doctor accompany Reid night and day for two weeks, but the hapless medic succumbed to the actor's effortless charm and reported that all was well.

But the truth could no longer be hidden. Reid's was one of 117 names to appear on the privately circulated 'Doom Book', compiled with the approval of Will Hays, President of the Motion Picture Producers and Distributors Association, the man appointed to clean up Hollywood in the wake of the Arbuckle scandal. The 'Doom Book's contents were leaked to the press, and the tabloid *GraphiC* splashed a story about 'Hollywood Hop Heads', which pointed the finger at a 'certain male star at Paramount'.

The studio finally went public with the shocking announcement that 'Good Time' Wally was a drug addict, battling his affliction in a private clinic. The sanctimonious Hays appealed to the public not to censure or shun Reid, but to regard him as a 'diseased person'.

The horribly debilitated star died in the arms of his actress wife Florence on 18 January 1923. Billed as 'Mrs Wallace Reid', she later that year supervised and played in *Human Wreckage*, a film based on her husband's experiences as an addict. One of Wally's big hits had been *Double Speed* (1919), a title which would subsequently take on a macabre double meaning.

'The Girl Who Was Too Beautiful'

A star who slipped through the 'Doom Book' net, and thus escaped the attentions of the foot-in-the-studio-door journalists, was Barbara LaMarr, an exquisite Southern Belle who was one of Louis B. Mayer's favourite leading ladies. The fan magazines dubbed her 'The Girl Who is Too Beautiful'. But she was not too virtuous. Life in the fast lane brought LaMarr six husbands, a battalion of lovers and death from an overdose of heroin at the age of 26.

The studio blamed it all on a strenuous diet. Like the heroine in one of her films, *The White Moth* (1924), LaMarr had fluttered too close to the flames. She was soon forgotten, but achieved a kind of life after death in the 1930s when Louis B. Mayer, casting around for a name for his new Austrian star Hedwig Kiesler, remembered 'The Girl Who is Too Beautiful' and gave us all Hedy Lamarr.

Tough Luck Tootsies

Some stars lived to tell the tale of their addiction. Juanita Hansen, billed as 'The Original Mack Sennett Girl', became hooked while working on the Keystone lot. Soon she was paying $75 an ounce for her cocaine supply. She found her way into the 'Doom Book' when it was discovered that she had been seeking medical treatment for her addiction. End of career. But

Juanita was a survivor and made her comeback as the founder of the Juanita Hansen Foundation, waging a war on narcotics addiction just as doctors 'now crusade against syphilis', as she told the world's press.

There was no comeback for Alma Rubens, wife of Latin Lover Ricardo Cortez and star of *The Firefly of Tough Luck* (1917) and *The Price She Paid* (1924). The price Alma paid was public exposure when, in January 1929, astonished onlookers watched as she ran crazily down Hollywood Boulevard pursued by two men and shrieking that she had been kidnapped. Cornered in a gas station she flashed a knife at her 'kidnappers' who in reality were her doctor and a male nurse attempting to commit her to a private nursing home.

A hopeless heroin addict, Alma was locked in a vicious downward spiral which led to committal in a psychiatric ward of the Los Angeles General Hospital. She emerged to make a comeback bid on the stage in New York. But old habits die hard. In January 1931 Alma was arrested in San Diego's US Grant Hotel. Stitched into her dresses were 40 cubes of morphine. She was led away screaming that she had been framed.

In her last interview she told the *Los Angeles Examiner*: 'As long as my money held out I could get drugs. I was afraid to tell my mother, my best friends. My only desire has been to get drugs and take them in secrecy. If only I could get on my knees before the police or before a judge and beg them to make stiffer laws so that men will refuse to take any dirty dollars from the murderers who sell this poison and who escape punishment when caught by buying their way out.'

Dracula's Death Throes

For horror star Bela Lugosi the end was a long, lingering affair, a nightmare life-in-death caused by the morphine addiction which reduced cinema's darkly handsome Dracula to a virtually speechless wreck, shaking and shrunken, drifting through the outer limits of fringe film-making.

After his triumph in Tod Browning's *Dracula* in 1931, Lugosi was one of Universal Studios' most popular stars. But perhaps the greatest irony of his career was that almost as soon as he was established as the first big horror star of the talkies, Lugosi began to feel the clammy hand of poverty row on his shoulder. The films in which he appeared grew inexorably cheaper and the parts smaller. By the early 1940s, he was down among the dead men in Monogram and Producers Releasing Corporation (PRC) cheapies, wearily replaying Z-budget versions of his days of glory.

But grimmer ordeals lay in store, for now Lugosi was in the grip of drug addiction. The last years of his life were almost unendurable. Could anything be worse than *Bela Lugosi Meets a Brooklyn Gorilla* or *Mother Riley Meets the Vampire*, both made in 1952? Yes, for at the end of his days Lugosi could find work only with the egregious transvestite movie maverick Edward D. Wood. The budgets on Wood's films were strictly subliminal. The rubber octopus with which Lugosi wrestled feebly in *Bride of the Monster* (1956) was a mangy studio cast-off. But no matter, Lugosi was still working, after a fashion.

By now his body was awash with substances as outlandish as any he had administered on the screen in his horror heyday. According to Wood's associate, Charles Anderson, 'Lugosi was in bad shape by this time. He had gotten past the point of being affected by liquor, so he had to drink formaldehyde. Lugosi and Ed were very interesting to work with as a pair.'

Lugosi died in 1956, but this merciful release did not prevent him from making a pathetic posthumous appearance in Wood's *Plan 9 From Outer Space* (1959), often cited as the worst film ever made. Lugosi's swansong was no more than some randomly spliced footage of the shrivelled star tottering around outside his seedy home. He has no dialogue, rendered mute, perhaps, by contemplating the ruins of his career.

Bob Lets It All Hang Out

The 1939 classic *Reefer Madness* issued a stern warning to its sensation-seeking audiences that any monkeying around with marijuana would lead straight to drug-crazed abandon. 'Women Cry for It! Men Die for It!' the posters shrieked, employing the time-honoured mixture of prurience, titillation and moralistic humbug favoured by all the best exploitation merchants.

Not everyone took this message on board. In 1949 rising RKO star Robert Mitchum was arrested for possession of marijuana and sentenced to 60 days in jail. Bob had been relaxing with starlet Lila Leeds when Los Angeles's finest made the bust. Lila was not the kind of girl who looked a gift horse in the mouth and grabbed the chance of the free publicity with both claws, starring in a rock-bottom cheapie called *Wild Weed* which was rushed out to cash in on Mitchum's disgrace.

But it was the luckless Leeds who bought herself a one-way ticket to Palookaville. Far from being wrecked, Mitchum's career went from strength to strength. The drugs bust helped to cement his rebellious 'Go To Hell' image, and by the early 1950s he was RKO's biggest asset. The public knew he was a naughty boy, and wanted him to stay that way.

Bob Mitchum and attorney Jerry Geisler react to Bob's sentence.

Cary Takes a Trip

In the 1950s the major studios attempted to woo back their disappearing audiences with films exploring themes which had previously been considered *risqué* or taboo. High on the list were movies dealing with drug addiction, among them *The Man With the Golden Arm* (1956), *Monkey on My Back* (1957) and *A Hatful of Rain* (1957). Drug-taking in the plush groves of Beverly Hills took an upward swing in the following decade. Even suave Cary Grant experimented with LSD, revealing a Jekyll and Hyde personality beneath the smooth exterior. The Jekyll character was the one on the screen, while Mr Hyde emerged off the set when the star of *Notorious* (1946) and *To Catch a Thief* (1955) was 'tripping'.

Notable drug users of the time were Dennis Hopper, Jack Nicholson and Peter Fonda, the stars of *Easy Rider* (1969), who took the psychedelic scenic route when making the decade's definitive 'road movie'. As the Swinging Sixties slid into the Sour Seventies, cocaine made a comeback even bigger than Gloria Swanson's in *Sunset Boulevard* (1950). The effects were noticeable on the screen.

In 1978 Jack Nicholson, a heavy cocaine user, directed and starred in *Goin' South*, a rambling comedy Western. Much cocaine was snorted during filming. When *Goin' South* was released, *Time* magazine's film reviewer referred to Nicholson's 'somewhat stoned eyes'. The *Los Angeles Tribune*'s Charles Champlin observed: 'Somewhat confusingly, Jack Nicholson plays the whole role like the before half of a Dristan commercial, with nasal passages blocked. Why, I don't know, and don't care to ask.' Message received and understood.

Fat Man Overboard

Making his movie debut in *Goin' South*, as a crazed Mexican deputy sheriff, was John Belushi. At the beginning of his film career, Belushi was already a doomed man, with a drug habit which gave the Hollywood of the 1980s a cautionary tale to rival all those of the Roaring Twenties rolled together.

An anarchic meatball of a man, Belushi had shot to fame in the TV comedy show 'Saturday Night Live'. The movies beckoned, and after *Goin' South* Belushi had a huge hit as Bluto, the animalistic campus slob in John Landis's *National Lampoon's Animal House* (1978). In real life Belushi was Bluto writ large: glutton, casual trasher of houses and apartments, and consumer of a fearsome amount of cocaine mixed with Quaaludes to take the edge off the cocaine high. Belushi took the drugs to fuel his fragile, complex talent, but they dulled his genius and hurried him along to the final fade-out.

After the smash-hit success of *Animal House*, Belushi was like an express train, careering towards the buffers at the end of the line. He thought he could snort the world up his nose and still keep up the pace. But by the time he was filming *The Blues Brothers* (1980) he was a physical wreck, holed up in his caravan on location in a stupor, pools of urine on the floor mingling with the brandy from an upended Courvoisier bottle, a mound of cocaine on the table at his side. Director John Landis flushed the drugs down the toilet; off the set, hired 'enforcers' tried to keep one step ahead of Belushi in his ceaseless quest for stimulation. It was a hopeless task. Everyone he knew took drugs. On the set of *The Blues Brothers* his distraught wife Judy noted at least 25 regular users.

A Universal Studios doctor who examined Belushi during the filming of *The Blues Brothers* told the film's producer Robert K. Weiss that he had to get Belushi off drugs, adding as an afterthought that the studio might as well get as many films out of the stricken star as it could, because he had only two or three years left at the most. Shades of Wally Reid!

And ironically it was with Reid's studio, Paramount, that Belushi finally wobbled out of control. The ebullient, improvising comedian of 'Saturday Night Live' had become a balding swag-bellied hulk, unable to sleep, think or piece together the shards of a shattered life.

In happier days Belushi and his partner Dan Aykroyd had given riotous campus 'lectures' to earn quick dollars. At the beginning Aykroyd would always appear to announce that John couldn't begin until he had had his 'injection'. But the joke came true, with a vengeance. By now Belushi was mainlining heroin. Losing his moorings completely, he sank into the sleazy nether world of small-time drug pushers on Sunset Boulevard, one of whom, Cathy Smith, gave him his last injection hours before he died.

At the time Belushi was studying two new film projects, *The Joy of Sex* and *The Noble Rot*. There was precious little joy left in his life, and drugs had long since killed his sex drive. Perhaps *Noble Rot*, a film about the wine business, was more appropriate, for Belushi had been rotting away before his friends' eyes for months. He died alone on 5 March 1982 in the trash-plastered squalor of Bungalow No. 3 in Los Angeles's Chateau Marmont Hotel. That summer Belushi's actor friend Robin Williams found a sign by Belushi's grave on Martha's Vineyard. It read, 'He could have given us a lot more laughs, but noooooo'.

Man's Favourite Sport

In Hollywood they called it 'Subject A'. It has made the movies go round from the early days of the nickelodeon, when a coin in the slot gave you a brief glimpse of Fatima, the belly-dancing sensation of the 1896 Chicago World's Fair. Nowadays the abundant Fatima's jerky gyrations might seem pretty tame compared with the sly hilarities of Russ Meyer's heavy-breasted heroines, or the designer soft porn of *9½ Weeks* (1986), but sex will always remain in the eye of the beholder.

The infant film industry was quick to create its own sex symbols. In 1914 William Fox and his supremely inventive press agents transformed an obscure stage actress called Theodosia de Coppet into Theda Bara, the original 'vamp', the foundation of Fox's fortunes, and the first million-dollar star to be presented as the object of sexual fantasy. No matter that Theodosia was a dull homebody with a weight problem. The studio publicists worked overtime to fashion this unpromising material into the epitome of female wickedness.

An extravagant history was invented for her. Apparently she was born in the shadow of the Sphinx, the daughter of an Italian sculptor and a desert princess. Ancient hieroglyphs foretold her coming, and her very name was an anagram of 'Arab Death'. What else? Photographs showed Bara on all fours, drooling over the skeletons of her male victims. The 'wickedness' in her films was limited to much suggestive lolling around in overstuffed interiors, and some heavy staring and back-arching, but in those days that was enough to inflame a million fantasies of forbidden delights.

The colossal new mass audience for the movies remained ignorant of the morality of life in Hollywood. But their eyes were soon to be opened. As Anita Loos observed of Tinseltown in the 1920s: 'To place in the limelight a great number of people who ordinarily would be chambermaids and chauffeurs, and give them unlimited power and wealth, is bound to produce lively results.'

Fatty Takes a Flyer

At the height of his fame no-one considered Roscoe 'Fatty' Arbuckle a sex symbol. The roly-poly comic was simply one of the most popular and highly paid stars in the business. In 1917 he had signed with Joseph Schenck at $5,000 a week plus 25 per cent of the profits and complete

Fatty Arbuckle on set waiting his trial for murder.

artistic control over his films. Among those who were given their start in the movies by Arbuckle was Buster Keaton. In 1921 Fatty moved to Paramount to make full-length comedy features on a three-year, $3 million contract. The former plumber's assistant was now a multi-millionaire with a lifestyle to match, complete with a custom-made Pierce-Arrow the size of a tank fitted with a capacious cocktail cabinet. Fatty was on top of the world.

Then disaster struck. In the early 1920s Hollywood was still a horse and buggy town, slumbering around its dusty orange groves. For rest and relaxation of the more sophisticated kind, the movie colony motored north to San Francisco. On 3 September 1921 Arbuckle decided to celebrate his Paramount deal with a party in San Francisco's luxurious Hotel St Francis, where he booked three adjoining suites.

'He Hurt Me, Roscoe Hurt Me'

Forty-eight hours later, on Labor Day, the party was still in full swing. Among the revellers was a small-time former model and actress, Virginia Rappe, who had a reputation for shedding her clothes at the slightest opportunity and was notorious as the girl who had given crabs to half the men on the Keystone lot. Virginia had caught Arbuckle's roving eye when she won a 'Best Dressed Girl in Pictures' award. At about three in the afternoon the 330 lb (150 kg) comic, his pyjamas flapping around him, locked himself into a bedroom wtih Rappe. His parting words were, 'This is a chance I've waited for for a long time.'

Some time later the party was brought to a halt by Rappe's shrill screams. Fatty stumbled from the bedroom, grinning vacuously. Rappe, thrashing around in pain, her clothes torn to ribbons, was carried out groaning, 'He hurt me, Roscoe hurt me.' Five days later she died in the Pine Street Hospital. A post-mortem revealed that a ruptured bladder had led to the peritonitis which killed her.

A botched attempt at a cover-up failed, and the floodgates were opened. There were allegations of rape and a theatrically staged arrest of Arbuckle on a murder charge engineered by a politically ambitious District Attorney. Rumours spread that Arbuckle had violated Rappe with a champagne bottle. In Montana outraged cowpokes shot up a cinema showing an Arbuckle film. Three sensational manslaughter trials followed, submerging Fatty in a rising tide of innuendo.

No-one emerged with any credit. Rappe was revealed as a good-time girl, pregnant and suffering from venereal disease. Throughout the proceedings Arbuckle showed no sign of remorse. The first two juries failed to reach a verdict, but in March 1922 the third acquitted Arbuckle, putting it on record that: 'We feel that a great injustice has been done to him. . . Roscoe Arbuckle is entirely innocent and free from blame.'

But you only had to look at Arbuckle

to realize that, in many ways, he was far from innocent. Although he went free, prurient minds dwelt on images of the helpless young beauty at the mercy of the slavering beast. A writer for the Hearst newspaper chain, which had hounded Arbuckle throughout the trials, offered a sickening valedictory for Rappe: 'Little Virginia Rappe, "The Best Dressed Girl in the Movies", whose up-to-the-minute clothes have been the admiration and envy of thousands, today wears the oldest garment in the world. It is a shroud.'

The trials finished Arbuckle. In a sense, however, he was the victim of circumstances beyond those of Virginia Rappe's death. During the trial it was revealed that four years earlier Arbuckle and a number of top movie executives had been involved in another scandalous party which had been hushed up with some generous bribes. The studio bosses' own hypocrisy had been exposed, and this was unforgiveable. Arbuckle was tossed to the wolves.

After his acquittal Fatty sold his house and fleet of luxury cars to pay the lawyers' fees. Paramount withdrew his films from circulation and consigned two others recently completed to the vaults. It cost them a million dollars. According to Hollywood legend, Arbuckle's old friend Buster Keaton bankrolled the hapless comic and suggested that he direct, under the ironic pseudonym of Will B. Goode. As William B. Goodrich, Arbuckle's directing credits included a Marion Davies feature, *The Red Mill* (1927) and Eddie Cantor's *Special Delivery* (1927).

Seeking a comeback, he embarked on a disastrous vaudeville tour of Europe and was cruelly booed in Paris. Buster Keaton, who saw him at the time, realized that Fatty just wasn't funny any more. Warners threw him a lifeline, and he ended his days directing two-reelers. He died, broke and forgotten in New York in 1933.

In the wake of Fatty's fall from grace, Will Hays, President Harding's Postmaster General, was appointed as a kind of moral overseer of Hollywood. Studios began to insert 'morality clauses' into their contracts. When Dorothy Cummings signed to play the Virgin Mary in Cecil B. DeMille's *King of Kings* (1927), her contract stipulated that for seven years she was to live life in such a way as to 'prevent any degrading or besmirching' of the role she was about to portray on the screen. When she sued for divorce shortly afterwards, the 'morality clause' was held to be an infringement of personal liberty.

Clara's Love Balm Romance

No studio would have considered offering the part of the Virgin Mary to Clara Bow. Paramount's 'Jazz Baby' was the new emancipated woman, with that mysterious quality – 'It' – oozing from every pore of her ripe, sexy body and signalled by her saucer eyes and red hennaed hair. Fast young men swigged bootleg liquor from hip flasks decorated with her pouting face, while Bow herself barrelled down Wilshire Boulevard in her red roadster with a pair of lap dogs dyed red to match her hair.

The live-wire Bow made a relatively smooth transition to sound, in the appropriately titled *Wild Party* (1929), though her restless habit of dashing all over the set posed problems for the crude sound apparatus of the day. Then scandal struck. In 1930 she disclosed that she had paid off a doctor's wife for 'alienation of affections'. The doctor in question was one William Earl Pearson, who had been giving the tired and emotional star treatment of the most intimate kind for her 'nerves'. This early experiment in alternative medicine consisted of giving the naked Clara a nightly rub down in the privacy of the Chinese-style den in her Beverly Hills mansion. It cost Clara $30,000.

Madcap Clara then dumped another $14,000 in a Nevada Casino, running up the debt without realizing what she was doing. Worse was to follow. In 1931 Bow took her former secretary Daisy de Voe to court for theft and embezzlement. Daisy counter-attacked by producing hard evidence of Clara's penchant for booze, drugs and gigolos. Not content with exchanging torrid low body blows with a host of actors from Gary Cooper to Bela Lugosi, she had reputedly accommodated the University of Southern California's entire 'Thundering Herd' football team, which then included a good-looking hunk of a tackle with the unlikely name of Marion Morrison. Later he changed it to John Wayne.

Clara won the case, and Daisy went down for a year, but it was a Pyrrhic victory. The public turned its back on Bow, she suffered a nervous breakdown, and was dropped by Paramount. She made two sad attempts at a comeback before a losing battle with a weight problem forced her into retirement with her husband, cowboy star Rex Bell.

In her later years Bow became a virtual recluse. Every Christmas she sent a greetings card to gossip columnist Louella Parsons, on which was written in a spidery hand, 'Do you remember me?' In 1960 she emerged from obscurity to nominate Marilyn Monroe as the heir to her old title of 'It Girl'. Marilyn, an even more tragic star who, like Bow, was loved by the camera but not by life, was dead within two years. Bow outlived her successor, dying in 1965.

Big Jack

In the heyday of the studio system, movie moguls and top leading men exercised a *droit de seigneur* over their leading ladies, not least when they were young and impressionable ingenues. In 1924 there were few budding talents more delicious than the 17-year-old Mary Astor, on whom fell the glittering, slightly glazed eye of John Barrymore.

Superficially, Barrymore was at the height of his career, but the corrosive acid of dissipation was already beginning to score lines in the 'Great Profile' and eat away a memory made foggy by drink. This, and the ever-present need for money, had curtailed Barrymore's stage career and sent him hurrying to Hollywood and the welcoming arms and cheque book of Warner Brothers.

Captivated by Astor's ravishingly innocent beauty, Barrymore persuaded Warners to cast her as his leading lady in *Beau Brummel* (1924). The studio paid Astor $1,100; Barrymore paid her the compliment of giving her private drama tuition in his suite at the Biltmore Hotel. In Barrymore's book there was no such thing as a free drama lesson. Astor's parents – ex-teachers who were obsessed with making their daughter a movie star – made the ultimate sacrifice, leaving Barrymore to his amorous devices. It was like a scene from an 18th-century erotic novel: the ageing roué, the young virgin, and the compliant parents locking the bedroom door and then tiptoeing away.

Barrymore and Astor became lovers, but the Great Profile's delight in young flesh was soon transferred to the beautiful 20-year-old Dolores Costello, his co-star in *The Sea Beast* (1925) and later his wife. By the time Astor and Barrymore were teamed again, appropriately in *Don Juan* (1926), the matinée idol's ardour had cooled. Wriggling off the hook, he told the unhappy Astor not to fret, as he was 'just a son-of-a-bitch'.

Six years later Barrymore co-starred with the young Katharine Hepburn in *A Bill of Divorcement* (1932). Drink had continued to do all that it's supposed to do, and Barrymore was inching inexorably towards terminal decline. But he was still determined to play the Great Lover. It was Hepburn's movie debut, and her introduction to the hazards of film-making could hardly have been more illuminating for a newcomer.

Barrymore kicked off by giving young Kate the glaucous eye, and soon convinced himself that his co-star was returning the attention. As Barrymore later told the writer-director Garson Kanin, 'I'm *never* wrong about such things. I never have been. I said to her, "How about lunch?" She said, "Fine".' Barrymore had no intention of swapping pleasantries over the Vichyssoise. Once they were inside his dressing room, he locked the door and took off all his clothes. The director, George Cukor, was a stickler for timekeeping, and there was not a moment to be lost. But Hepburn stood rooted to the spot as Barrymore advanced to claim his prize. He made a grab at her, but she backed away and flattened herself against the wall, repelling her ardent leading man with the corncrake shriek, 'My father doesn't want me to have any babies!' Collapse of the detumescent Barrymore.

Dear Diary

By the mid-1930s Barrymore's erstwhile lover, Mary Astor, had matured into one of the finest actresses in Hollywood, at her best playing devious seductresses and demure bitches. Her two volumes of memoirs, published in the 1950s, reveal her as a woman with an intelligence and wit which marked her out from the Tinseltown vulgarians who controlled her career. But in her own words she was also 'sick, spoiled and selfish, prowling around like some animal seeking momentary satisfaction. Sexually I was out of control.'

In 1936, during a custody fight over her daughter with her second husband, Dr Franklyn Thorpe, newspapers began publishing what they claimed to be extracts from Astor's diary, retailing the torrid details of an affair with playwright George S. Kaufman. The diary had fallen into Thorpe's hands, and he had no moral scruples at all about using it to prove that Astor was an unfit mother of his child.

Some of the diary's entries left little to the imagination. After a tentative start, Astor and Kaufman took the plunge: 'Tuesday night we had dinner at Twenty-One, and on the way to see *Run Little Chillun* he did kiss me – and I don't think either of us remember much what the show was about. We played kneesies during the first two acts, my hand wasn't in my own lap during the third. . . It's been years since I've felt up a man in public, but I just got carried away. . . Afterwards we had a drink someplace and then went to a little flat in 73rd Street where we could be alone, and it was all very thrilling and beautiful. Once George lays down his glasses, he is *quite* a different man. His powers of recuperation are amazing, and we made love all night long. . . It all worked perfectly, and we shared our fourth climax at dawn. . .'

These feverish accounts reached their own climax with a passage which became famous. Of an adulterous week-end in Palm Springs, Astor wrote, 'Ah, desert night – with George's body plunging into mine, naked under the stars!'

Nor had the jealous husband, Dr Franklyn Thorpe, been an angel. During the trial it was revealed that his reaction to Mary's infidelity had been a wild spree with a succession of floozies from Busby Berkeley's chorus line.

In her 1959 autobiography, Astor claimed that the diary was an imaginative forgery. Certainly, the seething style, written in the heat of the moment, bears little resemblance to the star's recollections in tranquillity. Nevertheless, as Astor observed, it earned her the reputation of being 'the greatest nympho-courtesan since Pompadour'.

Notwithstanding the high jinks described so vividly in the diary, Mary kept her daughter and emerged unscathed from the scandal. Indeed, it boosted rather than damaged her career, and gave an extra edge to the queen bitches she played in *The Great Lie* (1941) and *The Maltese Falcon* (1941). And the diary that created all the fuss? In the trial the judge ruled it inadmissible as a 'mutilated document'. It was consigned to a vault and later incinerated.
Lust to Lust, Ashes to Ashes.

Outrageous Tallulah

Some stars pose as pillars of morality. Others don't give a damn. Carole Lombard swore like a trouper and was always one of the boys. Ann Sheridan was a heavy drinker whose unfailing hangover cure was to hire a Mexican band to serenade her as she went about her shaky morning toilette. But they both took second place to Tallulah Bankhead. Bankhead's gravel-throated greeting of 'DAAAAAHLING!' passed into the language, and her genius for scurrilous repartee was part of showbusiness folklore. Bette Davis's *monstre sacrée*, Margo Channing, in *All About Eve* (1950), bore more than a passing resemblance to Tallulah. When the film was released, the enraged Ms Bankhead told radio listeners to 'The Big Show', 'When I get hold of her, I'll tear every hair out of her moustache!'

Tallulah strove mightily to preserve a reputation for being 'as pure as the driven slush', although the effort sadly overshadowed her genuine talent as an actress. Thus the Tallulah we remember is the broad who, on encountering Otto Preminger and Marlene Dietrich in the Stork Club, greeted them in the only way she knew how. 'Daaahlings, I haven't seen you in a long time. Do you like my new breasts?' Purposefully unbuttoning her blouse, she displayed her surgically enhanced bosom to the pop-eyed diners and an unimpressed Dietrich. 'I've just had them done – aren't they marvellous?' Tallulah gushed before swaying off to her table.

In his memoirs of Hollywood, Garson Kanin described a remarkable Beverly Hills niterie whose customers were entertained by transvestite versions of Claudette Colbert, Ginger

Rogers and Paulette Goddard, all of whom were indistinguishable from the genuine article in all but one important respect. Presiding over proceedings was an inch-perfect imitation of Mae West. He doesn't mention a 'Tallulah', but one feels she should have been there.

Errol's Wicked, Wicked Ways

A wayward star who took a more serious view of her own shortcomings was Lupe Velez. In the early 1940s Lupe was the quintessential Mexican

Errol Flynn with his last girlfriend, 16-year-old Beverly Aadland.

leading lady. On the screen her hyperactive rhumba cavortings, fractured English, flared nostrils and outrageous mugging made Carmen Miranda look like Little Orphan Annie. Off the screen, her life had been devoted to stimulating, if imprudent, diversion, including a steamy romance with Gary Cooper and a marriage to Johnny Weissmuller which quickly turned into a non-stop public brawl.

For a time Lupe was a neighbour of Errol Flynn, a combustible combination which quickly ignited. Errol invited himself into Lupe's bedroom. Stripped and ready for action, he lay down on her extravagantly large bed. Silence descended but not the red hot Mexican tamale. After an interminable wait, Flynn levered himself up to see the penitent Velez on her knees and praying hard underneath a huge crucifix in the corner. At the end of her devotions she crossed herself three times before going down on Flynn.

In the late 1930s Flynn inherited the mantle of Barrymore. On the screen he was the most disarmingly dashing of all Robin Hoods, a lithe swashbuckler with a magnificently muscled body and a carefree smile. Off the set he was a man struggling to survive, an irritable drunk with brittle bones and haemorrhoids. However, he had a reputation as a philanderer to maintain, and set about the task with all the joyless determination of a Casanova.

Whenever his yacht *Sirocco* dropped anchor, boarding parties of local good-time girls would appear more quickly than the time it took Flynn to splice his mainbrace. Errol christened his crew 'Flynn's Flying Fuckers', awarding them a badge of honour – a metal image of an erect penis and testicles – to sport on their lapels. He kept a record of their daily and nightly conquests, marking the points on a scoreboard. Sex had been reduced to little more than physical jerks, performed by same.

He Died With His Socks On

Flynn's freebooting ways caught up with him in 1943 when he found himself in the dock on a charge of statutory rape. The suspicion remains that the whole affair was part of a shakedown of the studios by a number of highly placed bent cops. If it was, it backfired badly.

The 'victims' were two Hollywood groupies, Betty Hansen and Peggy Satterlee. Betty, whom the cops had initially picked up on a vagrancy charge, claimed that Flynn had had his way with her at a 'swim-and-sex' party; Peggy's story was that she had danced the hornpipe with Flynn on the *Sirocco* – in front of every porthole.

It soon became clear that the girls were, to say the least, no better than they ought to have been, and far from unwilling sexual companions. Under cross-examination by Flynn's lawyer, Jerry Geisler, Hansen admitted that she 'didn't have no objections' when it came to being balled by Robin Hood, and vouchsafed the information that the star made love with his socks on. Hollywood wags had a field day, pointing out that Flynn's last film had been *They Died With Their Boots On*.

The all-woman jury had no hesitation in acquitting Flynn, whose career suffered not a jot from the hilarious court-room revelations. 'In Like Flynn' became the catchword of the day, and in *Northern Pursuit* (1943), his next film, Flynn was able to joke about the whole sleazy affair. The best moment in the movie comes when Flynn assures his bride Julie Bishop that she is the only woman who ever meant anything to him, then turns to the camera and roguishly asks the audience. 'What am I saying?'

Standing Room Only

Booze, drugs and the haemorrhoids took their toll on Flynn. By the early 1950s he was a puffy shadow of his former self, but still grimly fulfilling his sexual quota, a haggard Stakhanovite toiling away at the coal-face of the libido. Drugs began to play an increasingly baleful part in Flynn's life. In 1953, while filming in Rome, Flynn contracted hepatitis from a dirty needle. In hospital he kept his pecker up with the aid of twice-daily visits from a couple of streetwalkers who administered oral sex. Champagne, strictly forbidden in Flynn's supposedly enfeebled condition, was concealed in the flower vase. The flowers died, and Flynn, now himself one of the living dead, was hurrying to keep them company.

Bottle-nosed, bleary and wasted, Flynn died of a heart attack in Vancouver in 1959. He was 50 years old, but the coroner who examined the corpse said that it seemed more like that of an old man. His last girlfriend, the 16-year-old Beverly Aadland, survived their affair with her virginity intact.

A Secret Life

This was the public Flynn, but there was a private and equally sad man who made regular trips to Mexico to satisfy his craving for pubescent girls and teenage boys. Flynn's homosexuality reflected his own confused notion of identity and found bizarre expression in an on-off affair with another mixed-up star, Tyrone Power.

It began in Acapulco in 1946 and was conducted in obscure motels and at the Hollywood home of Edmund Goulding, who had directed Flynn in *The Dawn Patrol* (1938). The strain of this secret life produced some curious side-effects, notably Flynn's habit of exhibiting himself, fully erect, to his strictly macho buddies. They might have found the performance less amusing had they known that one of Flynn's lovers had been the baby-faced 18-year-old Truman Capote, with whom Flynn had slept in New York in 1943. Years later Marilyn Monroe asked Capote if he had enjoyed the experience. Capote replied, 'If it hadn't been Flynn, I wouldn't have remembered it.'

HOLLYWOOD DEATH TRIP

It was the beginning of February 1922. The Arbuckle scandal was at its height as the hapless Roscoe faced his second manslaughter trial. William Randolph Hearst was claiming that Fatty's fate was selling more newspapers than had the sinking of the *Lusitania*. Hollywood, now the centre of America's fifth-ranking industry, was being painted as a latter-day Babylon, run by a bunch of drug-crazed, sex-mad libertines. But worse was to come, and once again it was the accident-prone Paramount Pictures which found itself in the eye of the storm.

Death of a Director

On the morning of 2 February a team of Los Angeles Police Department officers arrived at a bungalow court apartment on Alvarado Street in LA's Westlake district, then a smart residential area, lapped in the expensive calm which whispers success and money.

They had been called out to investigate a case of natural death, but the scene which greeted them as they entered Bungalow B was anything but calm. The place was a hive of bizarre activity. Two top executives from Famous Players Lasky, a subsidiary of Paramount, were burning papers in

William Desmond Taylor, the dead centre of a celebrated murder case.

the living room fireplace. The instantly recognizable figure of Mabel Normand, the only comedienne of the silent era to enjoy the popularity of a Chaplin or a Lloyd, was feverishly rummaging through the apartment's drawers. An even odder touch was added by the presence in the kitchen of Henry Peavey, a black servant, who was washing dishes, while in and out rushed a succession of unidentified individuals.

One individual who was taking no part in these proceedings was the man who had lived and died in Bungalow B. On the floor lay William Desmond Taylor, one of Paramount's top directors. His face was composed, his clothes carefully arranged; an overturned chair had tipped across his legs. For all the world it looked as if he had settled down for 40 winks. Beside him lay a monogrammed handkerchief, which was picked up by one of the investigators and placed on a cluttered bureau.

Initially there was complete confusion about the cause of Taylor's death. The police were told that a man claiming to be a doctor had walked in off the street, examined the body, informed the film folk that Taylor had died of a stomach haemorrhage and left. He was never identified.

Normand, the studio executives and Peavey confirmed that Taylor had suffered from stomach problems. On the more tricky question of what precisely they were all doing in Bungalow B, milling round Taylor's corpse, the Paramount men and Normand stated that they were retrieving personal letters and telegrams. Normand added that in her case it was 'to prevent terms of affection being misconstrued'. Later she admitted that she had visited Taylor the night before.

There was an even bigger surprise in store for the puzzled policemen. After clearing the bungalow of its uninvited guests, they turned to the body. As it was lifted on to a stretcher they saw a dark pool of blood on the floor. In Taylor's back there was a small, neat entry wound made by a bullet. Subsequent examination identified the weapon as a Smith and Wesson breaktop .38. The 50-year-old director had not succumbed to stomach cramps; he had been murdered.

The neighbours were questioned. One of them, Faith Cole MacLean, claimed that on the night of 1 February, at about 7.45, she had heard what sounded like a shot inside Bungalow B. Looking out of her window, she had seen a stranger wearing a cap and muffler leaving by the bungalow's front door. Later, under questioning, she said that she was no longer sure if the person she had seen was a man or a woman dressed as a man.

The Secret Life of Bungalow Bill

The newspapers revealed further astonishing details connected with the Taylor slaying. Searching through Taylor's study, a detective had taken a volume from the shelves – *White*

Stains, an erotic work by the necromancer and pornographer Aleister Crowley. When he riffled through its pages, a piece of pale pink notepaper, monogrammed MMM, fell to the floor. Beneath a picture of a butterfly were written the following words: 'Dearest – I Love You – I Love You – XXXXXXXXX – Yours Always! Mary.'

MMM were the initials of 22-year-old Mary Miles Minter, Paramount's million-dollar replacement for Mary Pickford and the star of a string of films directed by Taylor.

The police also discovered a cache of pornographic photographs showing Taylor indulging in a variety of sexual acts with a number of leading ladies. In a closet they found a pink nightgown also bearing the monogram MMM. Other closets contained racks of female lingerie, trophies it seemed of the sex life of a superstud.

Who Killed Cock Robin?

The list of suspects eventually swelled to over 300, but the hard core were easily identified. There was Henry Peavey, Taylor's camp valet, who had discovered the body on the morning of the 2nd, and who not long before had been arrested and charged with soliciting young boys in a nearby public park.

Then there was the shadowy figure of Edward F. Sands, who had been hired by Taylor as his secretary. On 12 July 1921, while Taylor was abroad, Sands had absconded with the director's sports car and $4,200 in petty cash. The car had been found abandoned, but Sands had disappeared. A rumour circulated that Sands was in fact Taylor's scapegrace younger brother, one Dennis Deane Tanner.

Finally there was Mary Miles Minter, self-confessedly infatuated with Taylor, and her monstrous mother Charlotte Shelby, a former actress and the archetypal 'movie mother', grasping, money-grubbing, insanely jealous of her daughter's success and yet determined to hang on to her meal ticket, no matter what the cost.

The investigations rapidly revealed that Taylor himself was a man of mystery. The elegant director, with his impeccable English upper-class accent, had been born William Deane Tanner in humble circumstances in Ireland. He had carved out a successful career in New York as an actor and then an antiques dealer before disappearing in 1908, leaving behind a wife and daughter. He resurfaced in Hollywood in 1913, quickly found work as an actor and then turned to directing. He was soon at the top of his profession, handling the tragic Wallace Reid, Mary Pickford and her successor at Paramount, Mary Miles Minter.

There were as many theories about the motive for murder as there were suspects. Taylor was reputedly involved in the peddling of narcotics; in another version he had fallen foul of a bootlegger (one of the items thoughtfully removed by the studio before the arrival of the police had been a large quantity of bootleg liquor); yet another theory revolved around a score settled by an enemy Taylor had made while serving in the British Army in 1918.

Inevitably the press shone the spotlight on Minter and her gorgon of a mother. It was well-known in movie circles that Charlotte Shelby was the owner of a Smith and Wesson .38, and that on several occasions she had waved it in the faces of those whom she suspected of harbouring lustful designs on her daughter. In fact she was already too late. Several years earlier one of Taylor's cronies, the director James Kirkwood, had conducted a woodland 'mock marriage' ceremony with the naïve 15-year-old Minter and then got her with child. Charlotte had procured an abortion.

Charlotte's alibi was that the entire family had been at home on the fateful night, reading through a script. This was confirmed by Carl Stockdale, an unemployed actor who had partnered Minter in one of her early pictures. Minter claimed that she had not seen Taylor for weeks. Nevertheless, a mass of circumstantial evidence pointed towards Shelby and Minter. But during the 12 months which followed the murder, Minter was questioned by the police only once and her pistol-packin' Momma not questioned at all. This was extremely curious as forensic examination of the jacket worn by Taylor on the night he was murdered revealed three blonde hairs which were positively identified as coming from the head of one Mary Miles Minter. Five years later the case was reopened, and once again mother and daughter found themselves the major suspects named by the press. They were exonerated from blame and declared innocent without a trial.

The Plot Thickens

Tragedy stalked in the wake of the Taylor killing. Henry Peavey died in a ghetto flophouse in 1937, claiming on his deathbed that a famous actress and her mother were the killers of his master. The body of the mysterious Sands was found six weeks after Taylor's death, floating down the Connecticut River, a self-inflicted bullet wound in his head. It seems that he was not Taylor's brother.

Mabel Normand, whose career was already on the skids at the time of the murder, was involved in a second scandal in 1923, when her chauffeur shot and wounded an alcoholic oil millionaire with her pistol. Then she was cited as a co-respondent in a divorce case. Her career petered out after a few sad two-reelers. In 1926 she married Lew Cody, who had been her leading man in *Mickey* (1918), one of her biggest hits. It was a doubly dismal affair – both of them were dead within a few years, Normand of drug addiction and tuberculosis and Cody of a heart ailment.

Minter's career had also been on the skids at the time of the murder, her confidence wrecked by the demands of her domineering mother. After six more pictures, Paramount bought out her contract for $350,000. She began to eat to console herself, and the charmingly innocent heroine of the early 1920s swelled into a vapid blonde barrage balloon of a woman, locked into endless litigation with her mother over the dwindling spoils of her brief time in the sun.

A Mystery Solved

The Taylor case was never closed, but there the matter might have rested, gathering dust as memories of the scandal became ever dimmer and those who were involved in it disappeared or died. Then fate intervened, over 60 years after Taylor had been shot in the back by a person or persons unknown.

King Vidor, who died in 1982, was one of Hollywood's greatest film-makers, the director of such silent classics as *The Big Parade* (1925) and extravagant epics like *Northwest Passage* (1939), *Duel in the Sun* (1948), *War and Peace* (1956) and *Solomon and Sheba* (1959).

In the 1960s Vidor was pushed aside by the brash new Young Turks of Hollywood. *Solomon and Sheba* was his last feature film. Thereafter his declining years were marked by a series of unrealized projects. And it was one of these which solved the Taylor mystery.

After Vidor's death, his official biographer, Sidney Kirkpatrick, began to sift through the mountain of material which the great director had left behind. One day Kirkpatrick stumbled on a locked strong box hidden behind the boiler on Vidor's deserted ranch. Inside there was a mass of scribbled notes, memos, diary entries, transcripts of interviews and private letters. They all related to the killing of William Desmond Taylor. Kirkpatrick pieced this jigsaw together to produce a fascinating book, *A Cast Of Killers*, which laid to rest the mysteries surrounding the director's death.

Sidelined by the film industry, Vidor had retreated into the past to assemble his last great project. As a young director in Hollywood, he had known many of the major characters in the drama. In 1967 he began his own investigations into the killing. They rapidly became an obsession, and in the process Vidor uncovered incontrovertible evidence of not one but two astonishing cover-ups.

The Truth is Revealed

William Desmond Taylor was not the ladies' man he appeared to be when the police opened his lingerie-crammed closets. He was a homosexual with a preference for young boys, who were procured for him by Henry Peavey. Peavey had almost certainly been arrested for soliciting while on a mission for his master.

Taylor entertained his young friends in a room near his home, ostensibly rented for Peavey to sleep in when he had to work late in Bungalow B. The studio, already enmired in the Arbuckle scandal, was well aware of Taylor's habits and moved quickly to limit the damage. The lingerie, the 'pornographic photographs' revealed in the press (but never subsequently seen), and Mary Miles Minter's nightgown were planted by the studio executives who arrived at his home before the police. Thus they secured his status as a legendary ladies' man.

In his investigations Vidor found many discrepancies between the newspaper reports of the events surrounding the murder and its aftermath, and the records in the police files he was allowed to examine. So much of the evidence referred to in the newspapers seemed to have disappeared, or to have never existed at all. The reason for this was simple – it had been destroyed.

At the centre of this tangled web was the Black Widow spider figure of Charlotte Shelby. There can now be little doubt that she was the killer. Like her hapless daughter, she was infatuated with Taylor, a passion which had not been reciprocated by the courtly closet queen.

On the night of 1 February 1922 the pathetic Mary Miles Minter had broken free from the clutches of her mother and rushed off to see Taylor. She must have arrived shortly before Mabel Normand dropped by, and was probably hidden upstairs by Taylor. Meanwhile the demented Charlotte was searching for her baby. She was watching Taylor's house when the doomed director escorted Normand to her car, giving her the chance to slip into Bungalow B. Here she was confronted with Mary Miles Minter emerging from her hiding-place. Taylor's fate was sealed, and he was gunned down in front of the terrified Minter's eyes. With all these comings and goings in the critical 15 minutes between 7.30 and 7.45 p.m., it was hardly surprising that neighbour, Faith Cole MacLean, was unsure about the sex of the 'man' leaving the bungalow after the fatal shot.

As we have already seen, Charlotte was not interviewed once by the police in the 12 months following the murder, and in the subsequent investigations, conducted by DA Thomas Lee Woolvine, she and her daughter were exonerated. For this she paid a heavy price. Vidor uncovered evidence that in the years following the murder she was making monthly payments of $200 to Carl Stockdale, the man who had proved her alibi. But Stockdale was just a bit player in the drama. Charlotte also had to buy the silence of three successive DAs, Woolvine, Asa Keyes and Burton Fitts. This cost her plenty, and provides the constant undertow in all the civil suits she fought for control of Mary's fortune. Charlotte needed the money to stuff into the pockets of three corrupt public servants.

Finally, 15 years after Taylor's death, the truth was blurted out in court by Mary's sister Margaret, whose marriage to Hugh Fillmore (the grandson of the US President Fillmore) had precipitated another interminable legal wrangle. In open court Margaret claimed that she had provided false testimony during the murder investigation and had further protected her mother from indictment by aiding her in secret conferences with DA Woolvine.

Between them Woolvine, Keyes and Fitts disposed of all the compromising evidence. At one point Leroy Sanderson, one of the LAPD's best detectives, was on the point of discovering the murder weapon. He had a hot tip that Charlotte Shelby's mother had been despatched to the family home in Louisiana with the Smith and Wesson and had thrown it into a bayou. Some neighbours had marked the spot. Sanderson was immediately taken off the case by Fitts. The monogrammed nightgown, Mary Miles Minter's hairs, the shells from the gun, the letters which Mabel Normand feared might be 'misconstrued', the stubs of the cheques made out to Stockdale – they all vanished.

Seemingly safe from indictment, Charlotte and her daughter slid into obscurity. Charlotte was supposed to have died on 13 March 1957 at her daughter's home in Santa Monica. The death certificate did not show the cause of death, and acquaintances continued to report sightings of Shelby, the latest in June 1960. One of Vidor's informants, the Oscar-winning art director George Hopkins, who had been present in Bungalow B on the morning of 2 February and who confirmed Taylor's homosexuality, described Charlotte as a 'vampire bat', sucking her helpless daughter dry. Was she something more, a real-life vampire, one of the undead? In 1967 Mary Miles Minter was still alive, living in seclusion in Santa Monica. She was to be the last person interviewed by Vidor in his morbid quest.

Whatever Happened to Charlotte Shelby?

Vidor's encounter with the forgotten star was like a scene from *Sunset Boulevard*. His first glimpse of Minter, as he stood at her front door, was a blurred face peering down at him from behind a grimy upstairs window. Vidor did not recognize the grotesquely obese figure who greeted him at the door. There were no tumbling blonde curls, only a greasy mass of grey wisps clinging to Mary's skull.

Inside the house the outside world was excluded by thick black curtains. In the stifling living room the dust of ages had settled on banks of bric-à-brac from Minter's days of glory – playbills, lobby cards, yellowing movie magazines. As she twittered away abstractedly, thoughts of Gloria Swanson's mad old movie queen Norma Desmond began to drift through Vidor's mind.

Confronted with Vidor's preliminary questions, Minter responded by reading him some of her 'poetry'. Vidor gently pressed her, but she grew increasingly agitated, racked with sobs at every mention of her mother. Pathetically she recalled her woodland 'mock marriage' to Kirkland. Vidor could stand no more, appalled by the sight of this husk of a woman stumbling around the airless room. As he stood up, he looked down at the sheets of 'poetry' which Minter had read to him. There was the now familiar butterfly motif on the notepaper. On the top sheet, in a fine copperplate hand, was written, 'Twisted by Knaves, by Charlotte Shelby'.

A sudden chill gripped the elderly director. Was Charlotte Shelby still alive, as some had claimed, lurking upstairs, still holding Mary's life in her claws? Even more horrible to contemplate, could the woman claiming to be Mary Miles Minter really be Charlotte Shelby? The scenario originally envisaged by Vidor had now assumed the flavour of Grand Guignol, stranded in a nightmare limbo between *Psycho* and *What Ever Happened to Baby Jane?* Vidor had not the stomach to climb the dusty stairs in search of what might have been the most terrible revelation of all. He left. Mary's parting words were, 'My mother killed everything I ever loved.'

Vidor never wrote his screenplay. Mary Miles Minter outlived him by two years, dying on 5 August 1984. To the end she was embroiled in legal actions revolving around the Taylor killing. In her later years she was robbed on at least three separate occasions. After one such robbery, in 1981, she was gagged, beaten and left for dead on her kitchen floor. As the journalist Adela Rogers St Johns observed, the initials MMM ultimately stood for 'Millions, Murder . . . and Misery'.

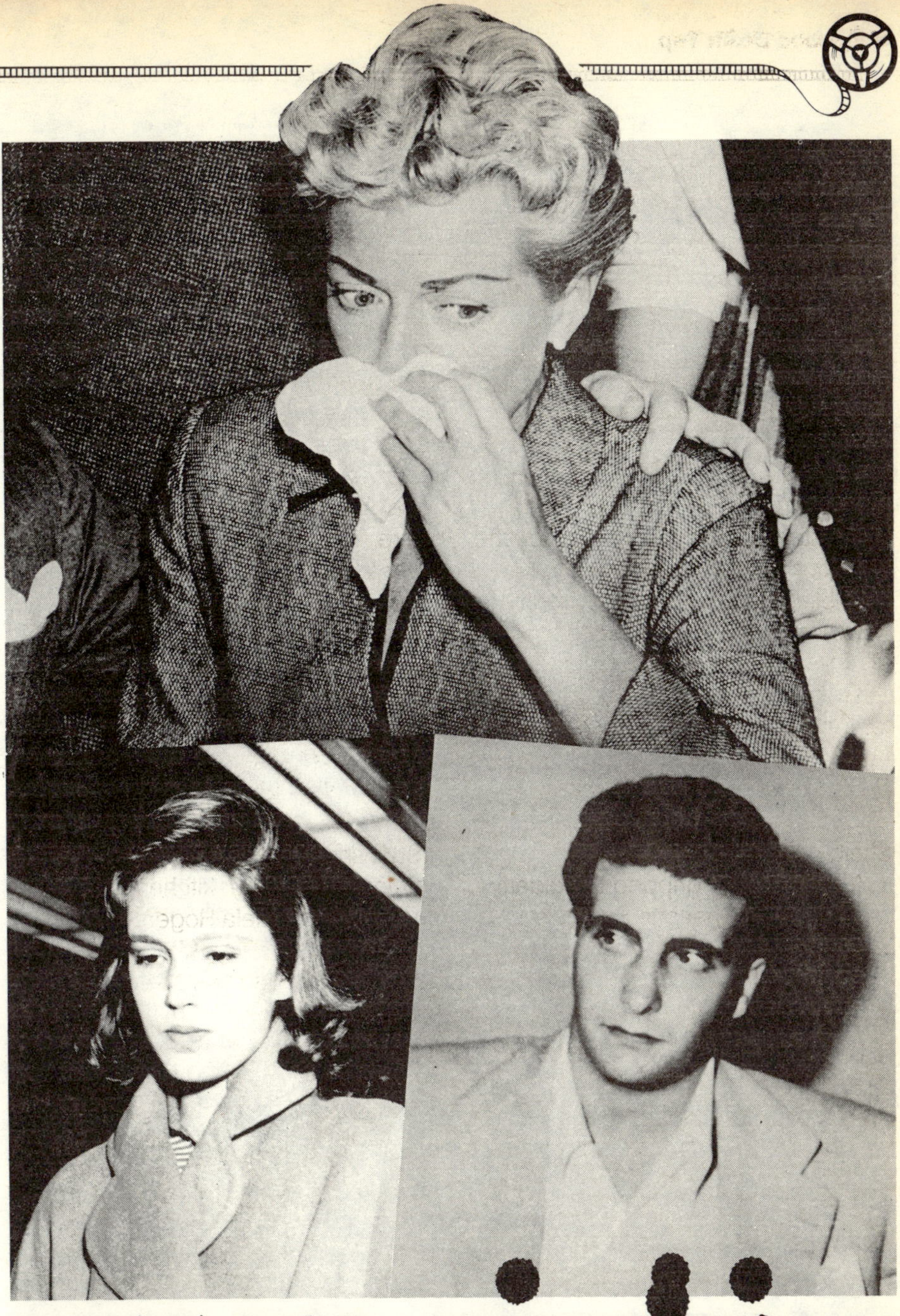

MURDER MOST FOUL

Top: Lana Turner in court; bottom left: Lana Turner's daughter Cheryl; and bottom right: Johnny Stompanato, Lana's murdered lover.

All Aboard the Lugger

In the early 1920s Thomas Ince was one of the most important – and self-important – men in Hollywood. He cast himself in the role of universal genius, a mantle later assumed by Orson Welles. In his brilliant comedy, *The Playhouse* (1921), Buster Keaton mocked Ince's galloping self-aggrandisement and his claims to story, production and direction on his films. Nevertheless, Ince was a pioneer, the promoter of stonefaced cowboy star William S. Hart and one of the founding fathers of the Western film. He was a man to be reckoned with.

In the autumn of 1924 Ince was approached by newspaper baron William Randolph Hearst, who wanted to lease space in Ince's Culver City studios for his own Cosmopolitan Pictures. As everyone in Hollywood knew, Cosmopolitan had been formed for the sole purpose of showcasing Hearst's mistress and protégée, Marion Davies, a talented comedienne but now better remembered as one of Hollywood's great party-throwers and a good-natured broad who never said no to a drink.

On 15 November 1924 the party was to be held on Hearst's luxury yacht *Oneida*, formerly the property of Kaiser Bill, who was now living in somewhat reduced circumstances in Holland. Among the guests were the British romantic novelist Elinor Glyn, who, when asked in the wake of the Arbuckle scandal what would happen next, replied, 'Whatever makes most money.' Also included were actresses Aileen Pringle, Seena Owen and Julianna Johnson; George H. Thomas, Thomas Ince's general manager; and Dr Daniel Carson Goodman, Cosmopolitan's head of West Coast production.

Marion Davies later stated that she was collected on the set of *Zander the Great*, at United Artists, by two individuals whose presence on the yacht has always been disputed – Charles Chaplin and the New York-based Hearst columnist Louella Parsons. They drove down to the yacht's moorings at San Pedro.

Oneida, packed with merrymakers and a jazz band, and loaded to the gunwhales with bootleg liquor, set sail, cruising south towards San Diego, where it was joined by Ince, the guest of honour, who had been delayed by a preview of *The Mirage*.

Thereafter a fogbank of confusion descended on the cruise of the good ship *Oneida*. According to the official version, carefully concocted by the Hearst newspapers, Ince suffered a fit of apoplexy brought on by a mammoth eating and drinking binge, prompted perhaps by the bracing sea air and the stimulating company. Dr Goodman made an on-the-spot diagnosis of 'acute indigestion'.

He was ferried ashore and placed aboard a train, accompanied by Dr Goodman. At Del Mar he was taken off the train and driven to the Del Mar Hotel, where he was examined by a Dr Truman Parker, who also called in another medic, Dr Horace Lazelle, for consultation. At first Ince attempted to protect Hearst by claiming that he had been taken ill while returning from a hunting trip to Mexico. Only under pressure did he disclose his true whereabouts and his consumption of an excessive amount of alcohol. The two doctors concluded that Ince was either suffering from a severe gastric disorder or a mild heart attack.

Later that day, Mrs Ince arrived with the family doctor and discharged the local physicians. On the following morning the stricken director was placed in a private railroad car attached to the Santa Fe express. At Los Angeles he was transferred to an ambulance and driven to his luxurious Spanish-style mansion, Dias Dorada, in Benedict Canyon. Within a few hours he was dead. The death certificate stated angina pectoris. No official inquest into Ince's death was held.

The revelation of the liquor aboard the yacht led to an investigation by the San Diego DA, which lasted all of 24 hours before the lawman was persuaded to think again. He stated: 'I began this investigation because of many rumours brought to my office regarding the case, and have considered them until today in order to definitely dispose of them. There will be no further investigation of stories of drinking on board the yacht. If there are to be, then they will have to be in Los Angeles County where presumably the liquor was secured. People interested in Ince's sudden death have continued to come to me with persistent reports and in order to satisfy them I did conduct an investigation. But after questioning the doctor and nurse who attended Mr Ince at Del Mar I am satisfied his death was from ordinary causes.' The DA's sigh of relief is almost audible.

Some Impromptu Brain Surgery

What were the 'rumours' to which the DA alluded as he sidestepped the legal quagmire threatening to engulf him? Even as Thomas Ince was being lowered into his grave, a story was running around Hollywood that he had been shot by Hearst with the diamond-studded revolver which the old brute kept aboard *Oneida* for target practice against any seagulls foolish enough to fly within range.

Hearst, it seemed, had discovered his beloved Marion exchanging low body blows with the hyperactive Chaplin in *Oneida*'s stateroom. Incandescent with rage, the movie queen's 'Big Daddy' had lumbered off to grab his popgun. Chaplin's legendary sex drive seemed set for an unscheduled, and possibly permanent, stop in the pits. Hearst returned, to be confronted by Ince. In the ensuing struggle the gun went off and Ince went down, shot through the head. Hearst was conspicuously absent from the film pioneer's funeral, while the complicated cover-up was set in motion.

It has often been suggested that Louella Parsons' uniquely powerful position in the Hearst empire flowed from Ince's death, which she had witnessed. The garrulous old trout had seen it all, but kept her trap shut. Ince's murder was her passport to the big time. Louella's biographer, George Eells, has written that Louella was never on the yacht when Ince was shot, but was writing her column in New York, 3,500 miles away. But a question mark still hovers over the last reel in Ince's short, crowded life. Could his attack of 'acute indigestion' have been exacerbated by a bullet?

One thing is sure. For ever afterwards the good ship *Oneida* was known by an entirely different name – 'William Randolph's Hearse'.

Death of a Latin Lover

No doubts clung to the murder of Ramon Novarro, the Mexican star built up by MGM as the successor to Rudolph Valentino.

Novarro reached his peak in the last great flowering of the silents. In 1926 he replaced George Walsh in the title role of *Ben-Hur*, his greatest success, and a year later starred opposite Norma Shearer in *The Student Prince*. His response to the arrival of the Talkies was a dramatically staged 'retreat' to a monastery. When he emerged from his contemplations, Latin Lovers just weren't the thing any more, and although he coped with the transition to sound, his career went quickly downhill. Novarro was essentially a figure of the 1920s, and by 1937 he was burlesquing his old image in *The Sheik Steps Out*. His film career came to an end with a cameo in *Heller in Pink Tights* (1960). Nine years later he met his own hellish end, battered to death by a pair of teenage hustlers, Paul and Tom Ferguson, as they ransacked his Hollywood home for the fortune they believed was hidden there. They finished him off by ramming a lead Art Deco dildo down his throat. It had been given to Novarro by Rudolph Valentino in the high summer of the silents.

B-Movie Madness

In the mid-1940s, one of the Kings of the Bs was leading man Tom Neal. Neal did most of the leading with his right, slugging it out in some of Hollywood's most celebrated nightclub punch-ups. The best-remembered was a knock-down and drag-out contest with Franchot Tone, himself no mean brawler, over the favours of Barbara Payton. Neal was no great shakes as an actor, but his romantic escapades and bar-room antics made tabloid headlines for years.

Partnered with Ann Savage at the 'Poverty Row' studio Producers Releasing Corporation, he formed one half of a low-rent but effective version of the A-feature teams which had audiences winding round the block: Tracy and Hepburn, Bogart and Bacall, Ladd and Lake.

Their most memorable collaboration was in *Detour* (1945), directed by the wizard of the subliminal budget Edgar G. Ulmer. In its bleak climax Neal accidentally strangles Savage with a telephone cord (see the film to find out how!). Twenty years later *Detour*'s bad dreams came true for Neal when he was convicted for the involuntary manslaughter by shooting of his last wife, Gale Bennett. Neal spent six years in prison. There were no comebacks. Eight months after his parole he was found dead in bed of 'natural causes'.

Cheryl and Johnny

In 1938 MGM launched a campaign to promote the 18-year-old Lana Turner as the 'Sweater Girl'. This was not because of her dexterity with a pair of knitting needles but because of her magnificent pair of breasts straining against the garment in question.

Lana exuded a vulgar, thoughtless carnality, like a small-town waitress with a dull face and a stunning body, waiting to be picked up by the travelling salesman with a cousin in casting. An appropriate image, as Lana herself had been discovered while working in a drugstore. She represented every shopgirl's dream – just a counter's width between obscurity and stardom.

Lana was at her best as the adulterous murderess in *The Postman Always Rings Twice* (1946), languorous in burning white and letting her lipstick roll slowly across the floor of a greasy diner to rest at the feet of doomed drifter John Garfield. Twelve years later murder stepped off the screen right into Lana's unhappy private life.

Oh, Johnny, Oh, Johnny, How You Can Love!

After the war Lana's fortunes declined. A string of marriages (Artie Shaw, Steve Crane, Bob Topping, Lex Barker) and affairs (Frank Sinatra, Tyrone Power, Howard Hughes, Fernando Lamas) were punctuated with violence, both public and private. Dark glasses often hid the bruises and weals which Lana had received at the hands of her men. She protested, 'I find men terribly exciting, and any girl who says she doesn't is an anemic old maid, a streetwalker or a saint.' But the troubled star seemed to find men most 'exciting' when they were beating up on her. Her tastes verged on the sado-masochistic. As she grew older, she required increasing doses of the shock treatment provided by her lovers.

In the spring of 1957 Lana was disengaging from her latest marriage, former Tarzan Lex Barker. She filled the gap in her life with Johnny Stompanato, alias Johnny Valentine, a smalltime hood, former bodyguard to gangster Mickey Cohen, and a gigolo with the reputation of being hung like a horse.

Johnny provided Lana with all the excitement she wanted, and plenty more. He quickly established the ground rules of the relationship: 'When I say HOP, you'll hop! When I say JUMP, you'll jump!' Lana hopped, skipped, jumped, and plenty more besides. If she got out of line, Stompanato threatened, 'I'll mutilate you, I'll hurt you so you'll be so repulsive you'll have to hide forever!'

Cut and Print

Lana lapped it up. When she went to England to film *Another Time, Another Place* (1958) with Barry Sullivan and a young pre-Bond Sean Connery, Johnny was shipped over and installed in her penthouse suite. He made a considerable nuisance of himself, appearing on the set brandishing a pistol and ordering Connery to stay away from Lana. Sean, a former seaman who knew how to handle himself, laid the former mobster out cold.

Stompanato was packed off back to Hollywood, where he made a much more sinister nuisance of himself, running up huge gambling debts and sexually abusing Lana's disturbed teenage daughter Cheryl Crane. And it was the unhappy Cheryl who finally took things into her own hands, quite literally and with gory results.

On 4 April 1958, listening outside her mother's bedroom door, she heard yet another bruising argument between Lana and her gangster lover. It reached a climax when Stompanato threatened to cut her up, adding for good measure, 'and your mother and daughter, too!'

The tormented Cheryl decided to do the cutting. She ran into the kitchen, reached for a nine-inch carving knife and proceeded to slice up the despicable Stompanato. It couldn't have happened to a nicer guy.

Later, in court, a near-hysterical Lana testified: 'Everything happened so quickly that I did not even see the knife in my daughter's hand. I thought that she had hit him in the stomach with her fist. Mr Stompanato [what ironic formality!] stumbled forward, turned around and fell on his back. He choked, his hands on his throat. I ran to him and lifted up his sweater. I saw the blood. . . He made a horrible noise in his throat. . . I tried to breathe air into his semi-open lips . . . my mouth against his. . . He was dying.' Hollywood's finest screenwriters could not have given the stricken Lana a more dynamite courtroom scene. She played it for all it was worth.

It took the jury only 20 minutes to reach a verdict of justifiable homicide. Hedda Hopper wrote, 'My heart bleeds for Cheryl.' The inquest had been a sensation. Mickey Cohen's men had discovered Lana's torrid love letters to Johnny at the latter's home. They were leaked to the press, who splashed them across their front pages, with the steamiest passages coyly excised. There had been nothing like it since Mary Astor's diaries had made headline news.

Predictably, Middle America rounded on Lana, whose sole supporter in the press was the shopsoiled knight errant Walter Winchell, who penned this cliché-clotted apologia for the falling star: 'She is made of rays of the sun, woven of blue eyes, honey-coloured hair and flowing curves. She is Lana Turner, goddess of the screen. But soon the magician leaves and the shadows take over. All the hidden cruelties appear. She is lashed by vicious reporting, flogged by editorials and threatened with being deprived of her child. And of course it is outraged virtue which screams the loudest. It seems sadistic to me to subject Lana to any more torment. No punishment that could be imagined could hurt her more than the memory of this nightmarish event. And she is condemned to live with this memory to the end of her days. . . In short, give your heart to the girl with the broken heart.' In short, Walt, pass the sick bag, pronto!

At Universal Studios the wily producer Ross Hunter scented the public's lust for sensation, just as a shark smells blood in the water, and cast Turner as the ambitious actress who neglects her daughter in Douglas Sirk's *Imitation of Life* (1959). Sirk brilliantly exploited Lana's hard plastic quality – in itself an ironic commentary on the title – and used her limited acting ability to give added resonance to her character's uneasy search for respectability. Thereafter Lana's looks became increasingly puffy, but *Imitation of Life* remains a fitting swansong to a career founded on a clinging sweater and a great pair of tits.

Stalk and Slash

Repulsion (1965), filmed in London by the young Polish director Roman Polanski, is a morbid inside-out version of *Psycho* (1960), charting with chilling technical virtuosity the descent into madness of a young Belgian girl (Catherine Deneuve) living in South Kensington. Her horror of sexuality drives her to batter her boyfriend to death and then slash her lecherous landlord to ribbons with a razor. We follow the journey into madness through her eyes, from the minutely observed obsession with cracks in the pavement, and the distorted view of domestic objects, to the terrifying hallucinations – hands thrusting through the walls of her apartment – which crowd in on Deneuve. A lingering image of *Repulsion* is that of a foetus-like skinned rabbit rotting away on the apartment's kitchen table.

One scene filmed by Polanski did not appear in the final version of *Repulsion*. Deneuve was to have claimed a third victim, a woman drowned in the bathtub containing the corpse of her boyfriend, seeping blood into the water. When the time came to shoot the scene, the actress Polanski had cast for the part could not be persuaded to put her head underwater. So Polanski grabbed a mackintosh and a blonde wig and played the part himself.

The story reveals much of Polanski's morbid nature, and the eerily comic side to his obsessive handling of violence and the sinister games people play with each other. In his films the violence is violence *observed*. Through his work runs a strong streak of voyeurism.

Polanski himself is the survivor of horrors such as few people encounter. In the war both his parents were sent to concentration camps. His mother died at Auschwitz.

By the winter of 1968 Polanski was an internationally famous film-maker, the director of *Rosemary's Baby*, a huge box-office success and the harbinger of the horror boom of the 1970s. In January 1968 he flew to London to marry the actress Sharon Tate, who had starred alongside Polanski in his elegant horror spoof, *Dance of the Vampires* (1967). The wedding reception was held at the Playboy Club, and the guest list reads like a roll call of the Swinging Sixties: Peter Sellers, Laurence Harvey, Rudolf Nureyev, Warren Beatty, Vidal Sassoon, Prince and Princess Radziwill, Kenneth Tynan, David Bailey, Brian Jones and Keith Richards. The blonde, petite Tate, who often referred to herself as 'sexy little me', told reporters that the reception was a very 'mod affair'.

Back in Los Angeles, the couple slipped easily into the laid-back, drug-laced lifestyle of the late 1960s. California was still basking in the bogus glow of hippy culture and 1967's 'summer of love'. But now there was a whiff of violence in the air. The Technicolor Dream was soon to end in disillusion and death.

In February 1969 the Polanskis moved into a large house in Cielo Drive, Benedict Canyon. Its previous occupant had been Terry Melcher, Doris Day's son. Shortly afterwards Polanski returned to London to work on a screenplay.

One day in March a hippy turned up at Tate's door asking for Terry Melcher. Theatrical agent Rudi Altobelli, the owner of the house, happened to be visiting. He recognized the short, slightly built hippy and sent him away. The man was Charles Manson.

End Game in Benedict Canyon

On the night of 8 August 1969 the eight-months pregnant Sharon Tate had several guests at the house in Cielo Drive. There was Wojtek Frykowski, an old friend of Polanski from his student days in Lodz. To all intents and purposes, Frykowski was unemployed, living off his friendship with Polanski and using drugs heavily. That night he was on the ninth successive day of a mescalin trip. Accompanying Frykowski was Abigail Folger, a wealthy 27-year-old coffee heiress. Finally there was the 26-year-old Jay Sebring, a fashionable hairdresser, to whom Sharon Tate had once been engaged.

They went out to dinner at the El Coyote restaurant. When they returned, Folger went to bed alone; Frykowski stretched out on the living room sofa, wrapping himself up in a Stars and Stripes flag; Sebring accompanied Sharon to her bedroom.

Outside Los Angeles, in the flyblown Spahn Movie Ranch, a ramshackle abandoned film set, another coyote was at work. Charles Manson, ex-jail bird and monstrous patriarch of the 'Family' who lived at the Ranch, had long harboured a grudge against Terry Melcher. He knew that Melcher was no longer living in the house in Cielo Drive, but ordered four members of the 'Family' to kill 'whoever was there'.

Into the night, along the freeways and down the backroads leading to Benedict Canyon drove 23-year-old Charles 'Tex' Watson, 21-year-old Susan Atkins, 21-year-old Patricia Krenwinkel and 20-year-old Linda Kasabian. They were armed with knives and a gun.

Arriving at the house in Cielo Drive, they cut the telephone wires and climbed over the wall into the grounds. Immediately they were dazzled by the oncoming headlights of a car. The car was driven by 18-year-old Steve Parent, a friend of the houseboy William Garretson, who lived in a cottage in the grounds. Parent's car was stopped and its driver shot four times. He was left slumped over the wheel as Manson's four assassins moved in on the house and its sleeping occupants.

Frykowski emerged fuzzily from sleep to find the intruders standing over him. Blearily he asked what was going on. Watson replied, 'I am the Devil. I'm here on the Devil's business.'

Even though he never fully threw off the drug-induced torpor in which he had fallen asleep, the burly Frykowski put up a desperate struggle before the killers got hold of him. Then the others were brought into the living room. Sharon Tate was wearing a bikini-style nightdress. Sebring struggled free and was immediately shot by Watson, who then announced, 'You're all going to die.'

Susan Atkins stabbed Frykowski six times as he fought frantically to break free. Watson followed him as he made a last desperate lunge to get outside, smashing him over the head with the butt of his gun. Then he turned back to Folger and Tate. Folger tried to buy her life with offers of money and credit cards. Tate begged her captors, 'All I want to do is have my baby.' Atkins told her, 'Woman, I have no mercy for you.' Folger managed to stumble through the back door, only to be overhauled and killed by Watson. 'Tex' then returned to complete his horrifying mission, stabbing Tate to death.

A white nylon rope was then knotted around the dead woman's neck and passed across a ceiling beam. At the other end it was tied round the hooded head of Sebring. The whole business had taken about 25 minutes. William Garretson slumbered on undisturbed in the caretaker's cottage. As a final touch, Susan Atkins smeared the word 'pigs' in blood on the front door of the house.

The bodies were discovered by the maid the following morning. Doctors rushed to the scene tried unsuccessfully to save Sharon Tate's baby. Sharon was buried on 13 August; alongside her was her 'perfectly formed' son. She was wearing a Puccini mini-dress. The 'mini', one of the fashion symbols of the Sixties, was a sadly ironic touch. For the murders in Cielo Drive had brought the curtain rattling down on the era of Peace and Love. Referring to the instant panic among Hollywood's drug-users, Richard Sylbert, the art director on *Rosemary's Baby*, told a friend, 'You can hear the toilets flushing all over Beverly Hills.' For Sylbert, 'that marked the end of the fun and games of the Sixties. . . It was the end of the joke.'

The Devil's Business

Charles Manson, the evil genius behind the blood-drenched carnage in the house in Cielo Drive, did not stay at large for long. In December 1969, Susan Atkins was imprisoned for another offence and confessed to a cellmate. Not only was Manson responsible for the Tate killings but also for two more murders, only 24 hours later, in which wealthy store-owner Leno LaBianca and his wife Rosemary were slashed to death and the words 'Death to Pigs' scrawled in blood on their living room wall.

There is an eerie similarity between Manson and Carol Ledoux, the anti-heroine played by Catherine Deneuve in Polanski's 1965 movie, *Repulsion*. Manson, the social outcast, and the serenely beautiful Ledoux, whose outer calm conceals inner chaos, have both been so 'imposed upon' – by others and by society – that they can only reassert themselves through murder. It is almost as if Manson was the ghastly physical embodiment of the dark inner processes of Polanski's mind, summoned up like the Devil in *Rosemary's Baby*.

The director's immediate reaction to his wife's death was to seek to 'control' it in the only way he knew how, by posing for *Life* magazine in a staged photograph on the blood-splashed front porch, the door ajar, hinting at the hell within.

Echoes of the killings reverberated through Polanski's subsequent career. In 1971, while filming *Macbeth*, he came to the slaughter of Lady MacDuff and her children. As ever the perfectionist, Polanski himself applied 'red paint' to the face of a small girl playing one of the children. 'What's your name?' he asked as he went about his work. 'Sharon', was the answer. Perhaps the only way in which Roman Polanski can exorcise the murder of his wife and child is to make a film about it.

Thank Heaven for Little Girls

Polanski continued to live on the edge. He had long been notorious for his penchant for young girls – a passion which had been shared by Charlie Chaplin – and in 1977 he accepted an assignment from the French magazine *Vogue Hommes* to shoot a glossy photo spread of young girls of the world.

Polanski's subsequent champagne-splashed photo-session in Jack Nicholson's jacuzzi with a 13-year-old, knowing beyond her years, led to a six-count indictment by a Grand Jury, each count a felony:

Count 1: Furnishing a controlled substance to a minor;
Count 2: Committing a 'lewd and lascivious' act on a child, a 13-year-old girl;
Count 3: Unlawful sexual intercourse;
Count 4: 'Rape by use of drugs', including Quaalude and alcohol;
Count 5: 'perversion', 'copulating in the mouth . . . with the sexual organ' of the child;
Count 6: Sodomy

If convicted on all six, Polanski faced up to 50 years in prison. Out for the count.

In another of the grisly ironies which stalk through Polanski's life, the date for the trial was originally fixed for 9 August 1977, the eighth anniversary of Sharon Tate's murder. However, in a plea-bargaining arrangement, reached at the beginning of August, Polanski pleaded guilty to the least serious charge, that of 'unlawful sexual intercourse'. Convinced that the child would be stigmatized by the publicity surrounding the case, her father had concluded that the guilty plea by Polanski was a sufficient act of contrition.

There were other factors at play. The child's lawyer was worried about her rapid physical development since the incident. Maturing fast, she had developed breasts and would tower over the diminutive Polanski in court. Juries are instructed to put such things out of their minds, but the lawyer knew that it would make his job more difficult. For his part, Polanski's lawyer made an offer that his client would found and fund a theatre arts school for disadvantaged children, where he would also teach. This prompted a member of the prosecution team to observe, 'That would be a nifty place for a child molester!'

Polanski had little difficulty in charming his probation officer into writing a favourable report on him, but had no success with crusty Judge Laurence J. Rittenband, who eventually ruled: 'Although the prosecutrix was not an inexperienced girl, this of course is not a licence to the defendant, a man of the world, in his forties, to engage in an act of unlawful sexual intercourse with her. The law was designed for the protection of females under the age of eighteen years, and it is no defence to such a charge that the female might not have resisted the act.'

Polanski was sentenced to 90 days of diagnostic testing at the State Facility at Chino. A 90-day stay was granted to enable him to continue working on *Hurricane*, a Dino de Laurentiis production.

The director arrived at Chino on 16 December, and spent 42 days there, among inmates he later described as 'the scum of society'. In the meantime he had been dropped from *Hurricane*.

He emerged from prison on 27 January. Final sentencing was set for 1 February. Hopes that the time at Chino had settled Polanski's debt to society were dashed in the preparations for the final hearing. There is little doubt that the very sight of the film-maker was like a red rag to the bull-like Rittenband, who had been enraged by Polanski's open flaunting of his relationship with the 16-year-old Nastassia Kinski throughout the whole saga. In chambers on 30 January he informed Polanski's lawyer that he intended to send the director back to jail for another 48 days, and this only if he agreed voluntarily to deportation after release. Otherwise he would stay in jail.

On 31 January Polanski drove to Los Angeles airport and took the last remaining seat on a British Airways flight to London. In the ensuing uproar Judge Rittenband overreached himself, telling reporters that because of his crime of 'moral turpitude', Polanski did not belong in America. Protesting that he was in no way biased or prejudiced against Polanski, Rittenband agreed to the reassignment of the case to another judge. No judge was nominated and the case was removed from the court calendar. No sentencing can take place until Polanski's return, something which he has shown no desire to do.

WHAT A WAY TO GO

W. C. Fields, celebrated Hollywood alcoholic, in characteristic pose.

In the good old days the final reel always delivered the goods. The bad men bit the dust; the scheming vamp got her come-uppance; the boy got the girl and together they rode off into the rays of a golden sunset. Hollywood liked happy endings, although it was easier to arrange them on the screen than in the frequently disordered lives of its stars. For many of them there was no heart-warming fade-out. 'Exit Screaming' might just as well have been stamped on the last page of their scripts.

In Tinseltown, clawing one's way to the top was merely the preliminary to the gruelling task of staying there. As she grew older, Joan Crawford's savage slash of a mouth and glaring basilisk eyes bore testimony to the strain of clinging to the top of the greasy pole. But few were gripped by a success drive as manic as that which scourged 'Mommie Dearest'. When profiles sagged or hardened into a mask of middle age, when breasts and bottoms drooped, hair fell out in handfulls and memories fogged, then the Dorian Gray world of the movie star fell apart.

Some Like it Hot

Drastic attempts to reverse the processes of Nature could have fatal results. In the Second World War Maria Montez had been the full-breasted queen of the Universal lot, the star of a series of incomparably garish 'tits and sand' fantasies which had scaled new peaks of high camp. Six years later La Montez's career was in the doldrums and her ripe good looks smothered in folds of fat. The blubbery star tackled her weight problem with a punishing regime of hot saline baths. Too hot. She was horribly scalded in her last dip and died of a heart attack.

A similar fate overtook overweight character star Laird Cregar, one of the 1940's great crackpot heavies – in size and style – and an incomparable purveyor of highly strung menace and fastidious grossness. But 20th Century-Fox's fat man wanted to play Hamlet rather than Falstaff, a fatal ambition. He died in 1945, aged only 28, after reducing too heavily for surgery. His weakened heart could not take the strain.

Sometimes the prospect of ageing was just too much. Elfin Pier Angeli, the wistful Italian star of *Teresa* (1951) and *Somebody Up There Likes Me* (1956), never got over her affair with James Dean, a romance squashed by her disapproving mother. Pier contracted a disastrous marriage to singer Vic Damone, but was shattered by Dean's death. In 1971 she wrote to a friend: 'I'm so afraid to get old – for me being 40 is the beginning of old age . . . love is now behind me. Love died in a Porsche.' Angeli killed herself with an overdose of barbiturates in her Beverly Hills apartment on 11

September 1971. She was 39.

The stars' hang-ups about their ages usually tend to be coy rather than terminal. On occasion, however, the condition can produce galloping mania. In 1966 the 71-year-old silent star Corinne Griffith appeared in court asking for an annulment of her recent marriage. On the witness stand, she claimed that the real Corinne was dead and that she was a look-alike aged 'approximately 51'.

Hollywood Junkyard

Impending obsolescence was the bogeyman waiting around the corner of every film career. It could be hastened by the passage of time, most cruelly for child stars, who were often professionally senile by the age of 12. Changing fashion could blight a career. Today's Jazz Baby, muscle-bound Surf God or mammoth-breasted Love Goddess are tomorrow's unemployable 'celebrities', drifting rudderless in a limbo of low-rent chat shows, Z-grade exploitation movies and unread 'ghosted' autobiographies.

Hollywood often reserved its last cynical kick in the teeth for fading and intractable movie stars by casting them as . . . fading movie stars: John Barrymore, obliged to parody himself in *The Great Profile* (1940); Hedy Lamarr in *The Female Animal* (1957); Errol Flynn (as John Barrymore) in *Too Much Too Soon* (1958); and Victor Mature in *After the Fox* (1966). Pity poor Hedy, once the embodiment of MGM chic, reduced to scrapping with pug-faced Jane Powell over lantern-jawed George Nader – and losing out.

When the Talkies arrived, silent star Constance Talmadge gave her sister Norma some eminently sensible advice: 'Get out now and be thankful for the trust funds that Mama set up.' For those unwilling or unable to bow out gracefully, death sometimes came as a merciful release. In the late 1930s Hollywood was haunted by the sad figure of bankrupt silent star Charles Ray, who eked out a living with walk-ons and fantasies of a triumphant return. His death, following a wisdom tooth operation, spared him more suffering. A similar fate overtook Harry Langdon, who had been one of the biggest comedy stars of the late 1920s but five years later did not even merit an entry in *The Picturegoer's Who's Who*. In 1945 Langdon died in painful obscurity, of a cerebral haemorrhage. His last film role was a bit-part in *Swingin' on a Rainbow* (1945).

End of the Rainbow

For others, death was perhaps the wisest of career decisions. Peritonitis carried away Rudolph Valentino, and a Porsche did for James Dean, freezing them for ever in the iconic attitudes of the Great Lover and the Rebel Without a Cause. No middle-aged decline threatens their legends.

Some, however, have staggered to the end of the rainbow to discover not a crock of gold but a crock of shit. Alcohol was John Barrymore's downfall. His dependency was such that in the late 1920s, when he was desperately trying to dry out, he was reduced to gulping the perfume from the bottles on his wife Dolores Costello's dressing table. Few stars have fallen so completely and from such a great height. In 1925 he was at his peak: a triumphant Hamlet on the London stage and, at 43, about to become a romantic swashbuckler to rival Douglas Fairbanks. Ten years later he was in the grip of alcoholism, his memory deserting him and the celebrated matinée idol looks which had earned him the nickname of 'The Great Profile' grown puffy and blurred.

In 1927 Barrymore moved to United Artists at a fee of $150,000 a film. As fast as the money came in he spent it. His rambling estate, 'Bella Vista', consisted of no fewer than 16 separate buildings containing 45 rooms. A dozen servants tended the two swimming pools, trout pond, bowling green, skeet-shooting range and aviary, whose exotic inhabitants included Barrymore's pet vulture Maloney.

Hard-drinking guests – of whom there was no shortage – could drown their sorrows in a replica English pub or a genuine frontier saloon shipped all the way from Alaska.

Barrymore transferred effortlessly to sound and stayed at the top for another five years. In 1932 five films netted him $375,000 and in MGM's *Grand Hotel*, opposite Greta Garbo, he gave one of the finest performances of his life. But drink was steadily taking its toll. He had developed a paunch and a dewlap under his chin; his glazed eyes were sinking into nests of wrinkles and his voice was becoming increasingly slurred.

In *Dinner at Eight* (1933) he came close to playing himself, a fading matinée idol. In the same year, drink finally exacted a terrible price. During the shooting of a scene for *Counsellor-at-Law* his memory deserted him; after 56 takes he still could not get it right. Next day he played it perfectly, but the writing was on the wall. There was a final brilliant flaring in Howard Hawks's *Twentieth Century* (1934). As Oscar Jaffe, egomaniac producer and ham supreme, Barrymore both celebrated and savaged the notion of 'great acting' in a relentless upstaging contest with Carole Lombard. Then alcohol took over completely.

By the end of the decade Barrymore had been relegated to supporting roles and leads in B-movies, his unfocused eyes gazing beyond the huge prompt cards held up for him to the ruins of his career. Occasionally he rallied. He gave a charming performance in *Midnight* (1939), although his co-star and former lover Mary Astor later recalled that throughout production he had little or no idea what the film was about.

It was a last flicker of the old genius before a sardonic descent into self-parody in a grisly touring play, *My Dear Children*, co-starring his fourth wife, Elaine Barry. Audiences flocked to see Barrymore fluff his lines and fall over the furniture. *My Dear Children* was a production as horrendously inept as Peter O'Toole's *Macbeth* and, with grim irony, as financially successful.

Director Otto Preminger was involved in the production of *My Dear Children*, and in his autobiography he left a vivid picture of the wayward Barrymore in his declining years. Word reached New York from the Mid-West that Barrymore was wobbling out of control. Preminger flew out: 'When we arrived at our destination, Barrymore was waiting for us at the airport, accompanied by the male nurse we had hired to keep him from drinking. Each of them had a bottle sticking out of his coat pocket.'

Preminger was horrified by Barrymore's physical condition. In Chicago he had decided to take up lodgings in a whorehouse, emerging unshaven and hung-over for work. On stage he spent the entire play slumped on a bench centre stage, the action flowing around him, seemingly oblivious to his and the other actors' lines. When the curtain went down for the intermission, Barrymore was too exhausted to be moved. For Preminger, the performance 'went on forever'. On a subsequent night Barrymore's excesses meant that the final curtain did not fall until one in the morning. The audience didn't care. They had come to see Barrymore playing a drunken clown and he was obliging them.

When Preminger taxed Barrymore with his 'abominable' behaviour, the Great Profile replied, 'Well, come tomorrow.' The next night Barrymore was impeccable and word perfect. In his dressing room Preminger asked him, 'Jack, why can't you do this every night?' Grinning broadly, Barrymore replied, 'B-O-R-E-D, my dear boy, bored.'

20th Century-Fox refashioned *My Dear Children* into *The Great Profile* (1940), casting Barrymore as a broken-down old ham actor. His last film was the wretched *Playmates* (1941), co-starring with another doomed Hollywood has-been, Lupe Velez. When the time came for a scene in which Barrymore was to recite Hamlet's soliloquy, the theatre's once-great Prince of Denmark couldn't remember his lines. Turning away from the crew, he mumbled, 'It's been a long time.'

To keep the bailiffs at bay, Barrymore played stooge to guests like Groucho Marx on Rudy Vallee's radio show. One night Mary Astor spotted him alone in the corridor of the radio studio, sagging against a wall like someone 'who just couldn't walk another step'.

Barrymore died penniless in 1942. Sad as it was, his disintegration had been mitigated by a talent for self-mockery which was evident even after his death. There is a famous story, told by Errol Flynn and David Niven – and later fictionally recreated in the film *SOB* (1981) – that when Barrymore died his old drinking companion Flynn went out on a binge to drown his grief. Returning home considerably the worse for wear, he found Barrymore sitting in his customary chair with a fully charged glass in his hand. On closer inspection the thunderstruck Flynn discovered that his old partner in crime had not, in fact, risen from the grave. Barrymore's corpse was on loan from a bribed undertaker.

The story has a sad coda. Twenty-six years later Flynn, by then himself one of the living dead, was hired to play Barrymore in *Too Much Too Soon* (1958). He's just about the only good thing in the film. When Flynn died a year later, there was no one around to play high kinks with his decomposing corpse. Errol had passed way beyond a joke.

Hairless in Gaza

Even alive and kicking John Gilbert had none of Barrymore's posthumous talent to amuse. After the death of Rudolph Valentino in 1926, Gilbert had become the silent screen's most popular romantic leading man. He had a big nose and rather close-set eyes, but his piercing gaze, flashing smile, and hint of vulnerability beneath the glittering exterior, were an irresistible combination. The sexual chemistry which crackled in his screen romances with Greta Gabo in *Love* (1927), *Flesh and the Devil* and *A Woman of Affairs* (both 1928) led to a brief, celebrated romance which prompted columnist Walter Winchell to coin the phrase 'Garbo-Gilberting' as a convenient shorthand for torrid affairs.

For all his romantic appeal, Gilbert was a man seemingly utterly devoid of a sense of humour. He lived his life through his films. If he was playing a Cossack prince, Gilbert would fill his Hollywood home with balalaika orchestras and serve his guests Beluga caviar. He submerged his volatile personality beneath these operatic gestures without any irony. He was as movie-struck as his adoring fans.

When sound arrived, he appeared with Norma Shearer in *The Hollywood Revue of 1929*, lending a laconic touch to a cod version of the balcony scene from 'Romeo and Juliet', and revealing a pleasant middle-range voice. Then came the real test in *His Glorious Night* (1929), his first talkie feature, which was released shortly after he had signed a new $2 million contract with MGM. *His Glorious Night* was a disaster. The silent conventions of the film were completely at odds with the addition of sound. Gilbert's intense, passionate style – so electric at its peak – now seemed faintly absurd. Audiences snickered as he breathlessly whispered, 'I love you, I love you, I love you' to a wooden Catherine Dale Owen. The Great Lover had loved and lost.

His next, the turgid *Redemption* (filmed before *His Glorious Night* and adapted from Tolstoy's 'The Living Corpse') died at the box-office. Tension had forced Gilbert's voice, perfectly adequate in *The Hollywood Review of 1929*, into a higher register technicians called 'white'.

When *Redemption* was released in 1930, Gilbert was well on the way to becoming a living corpse himself. He had thrown himself into his final role – that of tragic failure – and took to drinking heavily. MGM did little to help him adapt his bravura style to the more naturalistic requirements of the early 1930s. Gilbert had earned the undying enmity of Louis B. Mayer after becoming the unwitting dupe in a scheme hatched by Nicholas Schenck to sell off part of MGM to William Fox over Mayer's head. His contract ran out in 1933 with Tod Browning's *Fast Workers* (1933).

A few months later he returned to MGM on the insistence of Greta Garbo to play opposite her in *Queen Christina* (1933). It was a pairing born of sentiment, but a melancholy feeling clings to the film, and all the confidence and attack which Gilbert had displayed six years earlier had drained away. He was then snapped up cheaply by Columbia to make *The Captain Hates the Sea* (1935), in which he gave an excellent performance but was billed below both Victor McLaglen and Walter Connolly.

Gilbert's marriage to Ina Claire had collapsed, and he was taken in and dried out by Marlene Dietrich, ever the solicitous hausfrau, who then set him up as her leading man in *Desire*, produced by Ernst Lubitsch. But having sailed through the screen test, Gilbert had a heart seizure in his swimming pool. He recovered but Lubitsch, happy to be rid of him, secured the services of Gary Cooper. The distraught Gilbert then burnt all his boats by begging Garbo to take him back. Marlene dropped him and took Cooper into her bed.

According to Gilbert's daughter Leatrice: 'Marlene was unable to resist Gary Cooper. The moment father found out he went to pieces again, and didn't stop drinking until the day he died. One day Marlene went over to play tennis with him at his house. He fell down in front of her with some kind of seizure, and the real shock was, much of his hair fell out. His hair lay on the court. I think she really panicked then and realized what she had done. Her guilt was terrible to see.'

Gilbert finally succumbed to a heart attack on 10 January 1936. Dietrich put on an Oscar-winning performance at the funeral, falling down sobbing in the aisle and then weeping all over Dolores Del Rio's shoulder. Shortly afterwards much of Gilbert's effects were auctioned off. Dietrich successfully bid for 30 of his bedsheets, but no one bought the Great Lover's bed.

The Bottom of the Bottle

One of the saddest tales in Hollywood is that of James Murray, picked by director King Vidor from a gaggle of extras to play the lead in *The Crowd* (1928), the last great silent movie made by MGM. Vidor's instinct had been correct; Murray was a gifted natural actor and gave a moving performance as the anonymous young husband and father struggling to support his family in the Big City. Murray was then cast opposite the rising young Joan Crawford in *Rose-Marie*, a project which was abandoned by the studio, as was Murray when heavy drinking made him unmanageable.

Within a few years he was back at the bottom of the heap, just another face in the crowd. In 1933 Vidor was accosted on Vine Street by an unshaven bum begging the price of a meal. It was an almost unrecognizable Murray. Vidor gave him $10 and took him to the Brown Derby, where Murray made straight for the bar. Impulsively, Vidor offered Murray the lead in his new film *Our Daily Bread*. There was one condition – he had to stay off the sauce. Knowing full well that he was too far gone, Murray rebuffed him and left. Vidor never saw him again.

Hollywood would doubtless have rewritten this scenario as a tearjerker, with the alcoholic Murray, redeemed by the love of a good director, stepping up to receive an Oscar, his white-haired old Mom dabbing her shining eyes in the front row of the audience. Life had drafted a different script. Three years later Murray's emaciated corpse was found floating in the Hudson River.

The incomparable W. C. Fields was quite happy to drink himself to death. Martini was his consuming passion, until it consumed him, and by 1935 he was on two quarts a day. It was said that when Fields travelled he needed three trunks – one for clothes and two for liquor. Wherever he went, whatever he did, there was always a drink in his hand. At home, if the Martini shaker ran dry, he would summon replenishments by blowing on a hunting horn.

Finally, he was persuaded to give up drinking for most of 1937, which proved just how ill he was. While he was in hospital, Carole Lombard presented him with a pig and a bicycle, a reference to a long, rambling and rude joke he had once told her. Perking up, Fields cycled down the clinic's corridors, the pig trotting behind.

The last, and wildest, of his comedies was *Never Give a Sucker an Even Break* (1941). At one point he suggested that the billing be changed to *Fields: Sucker*. The plot, his calculatedly incoherent farewell to the insanities of Hollywood, concerns the adventures which befall Fields after he drops a bottle of whisky from an aircraft and dives after it.

His alcoholism was now completely

out of control and complicated by polyneuritis. There were no more feature films, although Fields managed three cameo appearances in low-budget musicals, looking like a man pickled in gin. He died on Christmas Day 1946, with his sense of timing unimpaired – he had always professed to loathe the Yuletide season.

Buster Keaton, in the 1930s one of Hollywood's great drunks, was more durable. Ironically, the onset of Buster's alcoholism coincided with the period of his greatest creativity, the years between 1923 and 1928, during which he made *Our Hospitality*, *The Navigator*, *The General*, *The Cameraman* and *Spite Marriage*, among the greatest works of the silent cinema.

Fascinated by machinery, Buster always revelled in mechanical props, but when he was persuaded to join MGM in 1928, and relinquish his independence, he was confronted with a machine he could not control, a huge studio. After *Spite Marriage* there was a rapid falling away, accelerated by Buster's drinking, his own 'spite marriage' to the dull and snobbish Natalie Talmadge, and MGM's indifference to his genius.

At his peak Buster had been one of the most graceful of all silent stars, with a profile like a Cocteau cartoon. Four years later drink and disappointment had ravaged those beautiful features, making him old, old old. Even now, however, there was a certain black humour about the effects of the drinking. On a hunting trip with his actor friend William Collier in 1931, Keaton was accompanied by a nubile young Paramount starlet. On the first evening, after a wild ride in Buster's sand yacht, the two men stayed up drinking. Keaton never got to bed, and was still sitting up with a drink in his hand when Collier roused him just before dawn to go out shooting.

Crouched in the windswept hide, Keaton suddenly groaned, 'I've got to stand up! Listen – my legs – I've no circulation!' Then he yelled, 'It's killing me, help me!' As the two men staggered to their feet, the dim glow of Collier's flashlight fell on Buster's boots. They seemed unnaturally tight. Indeed, they were. At some point in the drunken day before, Keaton had put on his girlfriend's boots, but was so anaesthetized by liquor that he had remained oblivious to the mounting pain until it had become unendurable. In the end he had to be cut out of the boots with a knife.

At the beginning of 1933, while filming the ironically titled *What No Beer?* with Jimmy Durante, Buster disappeared from the MGM lot. He had flown to Mexico with a goodlooking nurse, Mae Scribbens, who specialized in the care of advanced alcoholics. She took good care of Buster. One morning in Mexico City, after a heavy night of drinking, he woke up to find her in bed with him. She and Buster were married in Ensenada, California, on 8 January – at a time when Buster was in the middle of a complete alcoholic blackout lasting several days. To the end of his life he could never remember a thing about the marriage.

Keaton was dropped by MGM shortly afterwards. He was cast out into the wilderness. The resourceful Mae kept their affairs afloat with some discreet prostitution. In an afternoon at the Biltmore Hotel she could make up to $100 with a series of calls on 'some of my good men friends'.

Somehow Buster survived. There were a couple of films in Europe, a string of comedy two-reelers, work as a gag-man for the Marx Brothers, who treated him abominably, and bit parts in B-movies, notably an enchanting cameo in Reginald LeBorg's *San Diego, I Love You* (1944); and a third, happy, marriage which lasted till his death in 1966.

After the Second World War the French rediscovered him, and he appeared in *Sunset Boulevard* (1950) – as one of the bridge-playing Hollywood 'waxworks' in Norma Desmond's mansion – and with Chaplin in *Limelight* (1952). He never wholly gave up drinking; to the end he would ask doctors, after a physical examination, if he could drink again. Some must have said yes, for he often did. His genius was finally recognized at the 1965 Venice Film Festival. Behind the cheers there remained a terrible sense of waste. When the cheering died away, Keaton observed, 'Sure it's great, but it's all 30 years too late.'

Sunset Boulevard Revisited

At the beginning of *Sunset Boulevard* the bullet-riddled body of Joe Gillis, played by William Holden, floats face downwards in Norma Desmond's swimming pool. Then, in one of cinema's most glorious conceits, the dead man takes up the narration. What story would Holden have told after being found in his Hollywood apartment several days after he died?

Holden entered the movies as a clean-cut all-American boy. In the 1950s he had been known as 'Golden Holden', a supremely reliable and bankable star, ruggedly good-looking in a commonplace kind of way – a handsome version of the guy who came to mend the television or served you at the gas station. By the end of the 1960s middle age and heavy drinking had seamed his face and pushed his eyes deeper into his skull – perfect for the role of the ageing outlaw leader in *The Wild Bunch* (1969).

Holden was ideally cast as the washed-up movie producer in *Fedora* (1978), Billy Wilder's intriguingly botched companion piece to *Sunset Boulevard* and a farewell to the old Hollywood. And he was well used by Blake Edwards in *SOB* (1981), a satire on modern-day movieland. He died in the same year, falling in his apartment after a solitary drinking session and bleeding to death.

The Suburbs of Hell

Few, if any, stars have pressed the self-destruct button with such gruesome finality as Frances Farmer. Howard Hawks, who directed her in *Come and Get It* (1938), recalled that Farmer had 'more talent than anyone I ever worked with'. A big, commanding blonde with a firm jaw and a marvellously husky voice, she was, for a brief moment, Paramount's hottest leading lady, but by the 1940s she had blown up on the launching pad and begun a descent into a 10-year nightmare in the lower depths of America's most horrifying mental institutions.

The problem for Paramount was that Farmer wouldn't play the Hollywood game. While the studio pleaded with her to adopt the sable and limousine style appropriate to a star, Farmer refused to give interviews, drove around Beverly Hills in an old jalopy and – worst crime of all – raised money for the Loyalists in the Spanish Civil War. Frances was a political activist – she had visited the Soviet Union in 1935 – and was quickly dubbed a dangerous pinko. But she lost her way when she discovered that radicals like Clifford Odets, with whom she had a disastrous affair, and his Group Theatre cronies, could be as cynically manipulative as the Hollywood vulgarians.

Paramount meted out B-movie punishment duty to Farmer, including *World Premiere* (1941) with a sozzled John Barrymore. Her last appearance on celluloid for 16 years came in a Fox costumer, *Son of Fury*, as a replacement for Maureen O'Hara. There was nowhere left for her to go but 'poverty row', and she began filming *No Escape* at Monogram. There could hardly have been a more prophetic title.

Frances's mental balance had already been unhinged by a deadly combination of amphetamines (to control her weight) and alcohol (to control her nerves). In October 1942, while en route to a party thrown by Deanna Durbin, she was arrested on a minor traffic violation and charged and convicted of drunken driving. Thereafter her life rapidly fell apart. Shortly afterwards she dislocated a studio hairdresser's jaw, then became separated from her sweater during a night club thrash and raced topless down Sunset Strip.

On 13 January 1943 Frances was dragged from her bed in the Knickerbocker Hotel, and in a Los Angeles night court charged with failing to report to her parole officer. All hell had broken loose from the moment when, in the LA police headquarters, she had signed her occupation as 'Cocksucker'. In court she screamed 'Rats! Rats! Rats!' at the assembled gentlemen of the press, abused the judge, threw an inkpot at him and vouchsafed the information: 'I drink everything I get,

Frances Farmer plunged the depths of insanity, helped by drugs and drink.

including benzedrine.'

Kicking and screaming, she was carried away and put in a straitjacket. Certified as 'mentally incompetent', the next seven years saw an appalling cycle of release and recommittal, engineered by her mother, during which she was subjected to insulin therapy, electro-convulsive treatment, hydrotherapy (a fancy name for immersion for hours on end in freezing water) and, in all probability, an unauthorized frontal lobotomy. At the Western State Mental Hospital, Washington, she was confined, naked and shaven-headed, in a ward for the incurably insane.

Frances was released in 1950, found work in a laundry and later married an engineer (her first marriage had been to actor Leif Erickson). The marriage did not take, and she settled down to a life of alcoholic seclusion in Eureka, California.

In 1957 she was spotted by a small-time agent, Lee Mikesell, who married her and coaxed her into a comeback of sorts, including an embarrassing appearance on 'This is Your Life'. She played in stock and made a film, *The Party Crashers* (1958), a Z-grade 'teen agony' quickie which featured another tragic Hollywood casualty, Bobby Driscoll. Divorced again, she hosted an afternoon TV show in Indianapolis devoted to B-movies, now seen in a rosy glow of nostalgia. It had been different in 1941. In the last years there was some peace, teaching at Purdue University and collaborating with her constant companion Jean Ratcliffe on an unreliable but moving autobiography, *Will There Really Be a Morning?*

Frances Farmer's tragic co-star in *The Party Crashers* (1958), Bobby Driscoll, was to suffer an even more gruesome fate. Driscoll had been one of the most irresistibly charming of child stars, a big money spinner for Walt Disney in *Song of the South* (1946), *Melody Time* (1948), in which Roy Rogers told him why coyotes howl, and *Treasure Island* (1950), as Jim Hawkins to Robert Newton's eye-rolling Long John Silver. He was also an accomplished natural actor, as he demonstrated in RKO's *The Window* (1949), directed by Ted Tetzlaff, playing a small boy, living in an East Side tenement, whose habit of spinning wild tales causes disbelief when he sees a real-life murder.

In 1953 Driscoll's was the voice of Disney's Peter Pan. Peter Pan never grew up, but Bobby did – usually screen death for child stars. The work dried up and the delightful little tot became a truculent teenager who in 1956 was booked on a narcotics charge.

The Party Crashers was his last attempt at a comeback. Thereafter he was locked into a vicious downward spiral: a 1960 charge of assault with a deadly weapon; 1961 arrests for robbing an animal clinic, forging cheques and narcotics offences. There followed a six-month stretch at the Narcotics Rehabilitation Center at the Chino State Penitentiary. Of his drugs habit, Bobby said, 'I started putting all my spare time in my arm.'

After his release from Chino there was a grim slide down to utter destitution among the derelicts of New York's Lower East Side, the setting for his triumph in *The Window*. On 30 March 1968 two children, playing near a deserted tenement, stumbled on the decomposing corpse of a young man surrounded by a pathetic litter of religious objects. The tracks of the hypodermic scarred his arms. Driscoll's body, unidentified until 19 months later, was buried in a pauper's grave.

There is a harrowing photograph of Bobby, taken on a winter's day shortly before his death. The chalky, swollen face belies his 31 years. It is childlike, as if Bobby was regressing to the days, long before, when he was the tiny king of Uncle Walt's studio.

Feasting with Panthers

Frances Farmer was by no means the only star crucified because of her radical politics. In the 1960s Jean Seberg, gamine star of *Saint Joan* (1957), *Bonjour Tristesse* (1958) and Jean-Luc Godard's cinematic milestone *Breathless* (1959) with Jean-Paul Belmondo, became deeply involved in the 'revolutionary' struggle being waged by the American Black Panther movement.

The FBI concocted a campaign to smear her, spreading rumours that she was pregnant by a Panther. In J. Edgar Hoover's office in Washington, the decision was taken to move in on Seberg: 'Jean Seberg has been a financial supporter of the Black Panther Party and should be neutralized. The current pregnancy by . . . while still married affords an opportunity for such effort.'

A tame journalist on the *Los Angeles Times* wrote a piece about an 'international movie star' who supported the Panthers and was expecting a child by one of its leaders. The article left no reader in any doubt that the star in question was Jean Seberg.

A tragic sequence of events then unreeled. Seberg's baby died at birth. In a macabre funeral ceremony at her home town in Iowa the little corpse was exhibited in a glass coffin so that all the world could see it was white. Seberg drifted into a state of paranoia. There were repeated suicide attempts, divorce from her husband Romain Gary (a novelist, diplomat and sometime film director) and two more failed marriages. The paranoia gobbled her up; she became convinced that her refrigerator was spying on her. Death came with an overdose of barbiturates at the beginning of September 1978. Her rotting body, wrapped in a blanket in the back of her car, was not discovered for over a week. Seberg had been well and truly 'neutralized' by the FBI's finest.

Bangs and Whimpers

Not content with being the most colourful cowboy star of them all, Tom Mix embellished his extravagant screen image with a largely fictitious account of his adventurous early life: Rough Rider, US Marshal, freedom fighter in the Boer War and in the Mexican Civil War of 1910. The legend was so persuasive that many reference books still record these wholly imaginary exploits as fact. In truth, Mix's army days ended in desertion, and his cowboy days were marked by an arrest for horse stealing.

King of the cowboy corral in the mid-1920s, Mix rode through an amiable fantasy of the West, sporting an increasingly outrageous wardrobe: huge white sombreros, embroidered shirts, skin-tight white pants studded with diamonds, and pearl-handled Colt .45s transformed him into a veritable Beau Brummel of the range. At the height of his popularity he was earning $20,000 a week and the profits of his films were keeping the Fox studio afloat. At the end of the mile-long drive to his palatial home, a big neon sign flashed his famous initials into the night.

By the early 1930s the lights had gone out and Mix had been reduced to touring with circuses. His last film was a tawdry Mascot serial, *The Miracle Rider* (1935).

Five years later, Mix died in a spectacular auto crash which might have come from one of his best films. His body was pulled from the wreckage unmarked and impeccably dressed, his pockets stuffed with cash and cheques. In the pile-up a metal suitcase had struck him on the back of the neck, killing him instantly. The last of the legends surrounding Mix's flamboyant life filled the case with a hoard of gold $20 pieces.

In 1931 the great German director F. W. Murnau rode to death in different fashion. When his car skidded off the road it was being driven by his 14-year-old Filipino manservant, to whom, it was rumoured, the homosexual director was paying some rather intimate and distracting attention. Only 11 mourners attended Murnau's funeral, among them Greta Garbo, who commissioned a death mask of the master director which she kept on her desk.

Here Come the Lizards

In 1967 Jayne Mansfield and her boyfriend-cum-manager Sam Brody were driving to a TV engagement near New Orleans. Their sports car slammed into a truck. The fading star and her lover were decapitated. In the crash, the mutilated body of Jayne's pet chihuahua was squirted out on to the tarmac.

The sheer horror of her end obscured the nightmarish last years of Mansfield's career. In the mid-1950s Hollywood wheeled out a new gimmick to win back the audiences lost to television – big boobs. In a class of her own was Jayne Mansfield, with eye-boggling measurements of 40-18½-36. She hit the big-time in 1956 when 20th Century-Fox, embroiled in a feud with the recalcitrant Marilyn Monroe, signed Jayne to a seven-year contract.

Director Frank Tashlin packaged her principal attributes in a raucous comedy, *The Girl Can't Help It*. Tashlin had started his career in 1928 as animator with Max Fleischer, and in Mansfield's absurd curves he found the closest human approximation to a 'cartoon woman', around whose anatomy he sprayed machine-gun bursts of mocking sight gags. The most celebrated was when Jayne appeared clutching a milk bottle in front of each pendulous breast, bringing a new dimension to the concept of 'Sign and Meaning in the Cinema'. Tashlin believed that 'there's nothing more hysterical to me than big-breasted women – like walking leaning towers'.

In the end, Jayne seems more pathetic than risible, let alone sexy. The thought of her completely unclothed is enough to make the strongest stomach churn. Remarkably, in *The Girl Can't Help It* she retains a touchingly sympathetic quality, telling Tom Ewell that she just wants to be a housewife and mother, and pretending that she can't sing in order to prevent her gangster boyfriend Marty 'Fats' Murdoch (Edmond O'Brien) from launching her on a showbiz career.

It was Jayne's 'showbiz career' which did her in. Inevitably, the shelf life of her oversized mammaries was limited. Even the most vigorously inflated balloons soon start to grow slack and wrinkled. By the early 1960s she was still making headlines, but her film appearances were now restricted to sleazy exploiters like *The Fat Spy* (1966), playing the daughter of another zonked-out Hollywood veteran, Brian Donlevy; and *L'Amore Primitivo* (1964), in which the flimsy plot required her to perform an extremely primitivo strip for a bug-eyed anthropologist and a couple of astonished hotel porters. There were rumours of a porno film and a list of weird unreleased movies, including *Dog Eat Dog* (1965), *Mondo Hollywood* (1967) and *The Wild, Wild World of Jayne Mansfield* (1967).

By then Jayne's world had progressed from the Wild to the Woolly and Way Beyond. When she sang 'Fly Me to the Moon' in her nightclub act, it was clear that she was zooming out of control through the outer limits of the universe. She was on Warp Factor 13, dabbling in Black Magic, sinking two bottles of Bourbon a day and gobbling fistfuls of diet pills to stay awake. Increasingly mountainous, she waddled around in a tiny miniskirt, her arms and thighs blotched with the livid bruises sustained in her frequent

Jayne Mansfield, with Sophia Loren, revealing two of her assets.

brawls with the loathsome Brody. Behind them the happy couple left a trail of bottle-strewn hotel suites caked in the excrement of Jayne's yapping pet dogs.

In one sense at least, her wild behaviour was an expression of disgust, both at what she had become and the predatory and brutal men who had exploited her and brought her to this pass. One night, during her nightclub act, she perched on the knees of an elderly man, yanked out a gigantic, flaccid breast and rammed the nipple into his gaping mouth.

In hospital just before her death, Jayne and Sam went bananas. Dropping LSD, gulping booze and guzzling uppers, they went on a rampage. Within a week the hospital administrator had died of a heart attack.

Mansfield's press secretary Raymond Strait has left a ghastly picture of the hellish pit into which she had sunk in her final days. Visiting Jayne and Sam at home, Strait had gone into the kitchen to mix himself a drink. Suddenly he heard a blood-curdling scream. Rushing back to Brody's leather-lined den, he was confronted by the sight of Jayne climbing the bookshelves, 'her throat filled with such screeching noises that she sounded more animal than human'. Over and over again she moaned, 'The lizards, the lizards! The fucking lizards! Look at them! Oh, my God, look at them!'

Clinging to the shelves with one hand, she jabbed a finger towards the desk. Then Strait saw Brody, crouched in the corner, his eyes set and glassy, masturbating frantically: 'His tongue kept flicking his lips as he hammered himself toward some incredible satisfaction.' All the while he crooned, 'Do it, baby, do it. Beautiful. Eat the little pussy. Little lizards eat the pussy!'

Strait reeled into the night. He never saw Mansfield again. If ever there was case of Dog Eat Dog in Mondo Hollywood it was that of Jayne Mansfield. The girl just couldn't help it.

Suicide Gulch

When a career crashed full tilt into the buffers at the end of the line, or simply failed to get started at all; when the phone stopped ringing and your agent always seemed to be 'out of town'; when your luck and your lovers flew out of the window, what was there left to do but make the final gesture, the final admission of the futility of it all!

There remained the small matter of choosing the method of self-disposal. In the best of all possible worlds, the last act should be skilfully stage managed.

Out-of-work British actress Peg Entwhistle carved her own little niche in cinema history when, on 8 September 1932, she flung herself off the 50ft-high letter 'H' in the giant Hollywoodland sign on Mount Lee. Her suicide note read, 'I'm afraid I'm a coward. I'm sorry for everything.'

So was Lupe Velez. This is the last time we will encounter the fiery little enchilada from south of the border and, appropriately, it is at the moment of her unintentionally spectacular demise.

In the last entry in her Mexican Spitfire series, *Mexican Spitfire's Blessed Event* (1943), she acquired an ocelot and became pregnant. Why are the titles of the last films of so many doomed stars so eerily prophetic? The great scriptwriter in the sky must have a peculiarly warped sense of humour. When Lupe became pregnant not long afterwards, there was no happy fadeout. Abandoned by her toyboy lover Harald Ramond, and saddled with huge debts, she now had to make a choice between abortion and the scandal that would grow as fast as her swelling belly. She decided to end it all – in style.

On the fatal night she ate an elaborate Mexican meal with two girlfriends, then returned to her fake hacienda on North Rodeo Drive. She mounted the stairs to her flower-filled bedroom, lit with the glow of candles. After writing a maudlin farewell letter to her faithless lover she then swallowed an entire bottle of Seconal.

Resplendent in her silver lamé evening gown, she lay on her outsize bed, beneath the huge crucifix on the wall – the one at which she had prayed so hard before fellating Errol Flynn. Doubtless she woozily pictured the obituaries Hedda and Louella would write as she slipped into the Big Sleep.

Next day Louella gushed: 'Lupe was never lovelier as she lay there, as if slumbering . . . A faint smile, like a good little girl . . . Hark! There are the doggies, there's Chops, there's Chips, scratching at the door . . . They're whimpering, they're whining . . . They want their little Lupita to take them out to play. . .'

Ah, the authentic touch of the mistress of mush. But not, it would seem, a wholly accurate account of events in the small hours at Casa Felicias on North Rodeo Drive. Lupita was not discovered lying on her bed like an abandoned china doll. That morning a trail of vile-smelling vomit led Lupe's maid to the bathroom. There she found La Velez, dead as mutton, her head rammed down the toilet bowl.

At some point after consuming the bottle of Seconal Lupe had drifted back into a nauseous consciousness. Instinctively, she had lurched for the bathroom, slipped on the tiles and taken a header into her Egyptian Chartreuse Onyx Hush-Flush Model Deluxe, where she drowned in her own vomit. One of the most accomplished Hollywood practitioners of fellatio had gone down for the last time, on herself.

Nothing was left to chance by Albert Dekker, the spooky character actor best remembered as the bullet-headed, pebble-spectacled Dr Thorkel, the mad scientist who shrinks his human victims in the glorious

Technicolor *Dr Cyclops* (1940). Bondage freak Dekker had long since become disillusioned with the vagaries of life in Tinseltown, telling critic Ward Morehouse: 'The theatre is a horrible place in which to make a living. They sit you on the shelf for years. They take you off and brush you off and later you have to find your way back to the shelf.'

Dekker jumped off the shelf on 5 May 1968, hanging himself in the bathroom of his Hollywood apartment. A common enough occurrence, perhaps, but there was a surprise waiting for the police who broke down the door.

Hanging on a shower rod was the paunchy Dekker, bedecked in frilly lingerie and suspenders, obscenities scrawled all over his puckered flesh in livid lipstick.

Bite the Bullet

From the 1919 case of 'Country Boy' actor Bobby Harron, who shot himself after being discarded by D. W. Griffith, there has been a long, sad list of Hollywood stars and mini-celebrities who have wound up looking down the barrel of a gun held in their own shaking hand. Among them are cowboy star Don 'Red' Barry; Jonathan Hale, Dagwood Bumstead's boss, Mr Dithers, in the long-running Blondie series; the original Superman, George Reeves, forever typecast as the Caped Crusader; heavyweight Czech character star Walter Slezak, depressed by a heart ailment; bedridden Jon Hall, once Maria Montez's muscular leading man in the camp classic *Cobra Woman* (1944); and art director Wilfred Buckland, who on 18 July 1946 shot and killed his gay, alcoholic son and then turned the gun on himself – Buckland was a skilled amateur marksman and did not miss his last target.

In the late 1920s Karl Dane had been a popular character actor at MGM, making his mark as Slim, John Gilbert's hard-bitten First World War buddy in *The Big Parade* (1925). Dane's big scene in the film comes when he is killed on a mission to rescue a wounded soldier in no-man's-land.

With the coming of sound, Dane was himself stranded in a cinematic no-man's land, his thick Danish accent bringing a premature end to his career. He was reduced to running a hot-dog stall near the gates of MGM's Culver City studios. On 14 April 1934 he shot himself in his dingy lodgings. Neighbours found his body surrounded by his yellowing press clippings.

Marriage to blonde bombshell Jean Harlow was all too much for Paul Bern, Irving Thalberg's intense, intellectual assistant at MGM. The studio's hottest property was 21 when they married, while Bern was 22 years her senior. The age difference was not the crucial factor so much as Bern's attempts to compensate for his lack of potency with an artificial rubber phallus. The marriage lasted a mere two months. On 5 September 1932 Bern shot himself in the couple's all-white bedroom in their Benedict Canyon mansion. He left a note for Harlow:

> Dearest Dear,
> Unfortunately this is the only way to make good the frightful wrong I have done you, and to wipe out my abject humiliation.
> Love you.
> Paul
> You understand that last night was only a comedy.

In the 1920s Clyde Bruckman had been one of the Hollywood 'in crowd', a writer-director for Buster Keaton, Harold Lloyd and Laurel and Hardy. In the 1930s alcoholism blighted his career, and by 1945 he was scratching a living by selling Universal recycled versions of the gags he had once dreamed up for Harold Lloyd. The multi-millionaire Lloyd took umbrage when his material turned up in a Joan Davis B-movie, *She Gets Her Man* (1945), and took Universal to the cleaners with a plagiarism suit. Bruckman's slender lifeline had been severed and he was left to survive on memories and booze.

In 1955 Bruckman borrowed a pistol from his old friend Buster Keaton for 'target practice'. He then walked into a smart restaurant, ordered a lavish meal, downed a coffee and brandy and shot himself.

Sadder by far was the death of suave character actor Gig Young. In *Come Fill the Cup* (1951) he had played a hopeless alcoholic reformed by James Cagney. In real-life Young himself was an alcoholic with a death wish which finally became unendurable.

Young won a Best Supporting Actor Oscar for his performances in *They Shoot Horses Don't They?* (1969). He is usually associated with elegantly self-effacing supporting roles, like playing deft second fiddle to Cary Grant in *That Touch of Mink* (1962). But a disturbingly powerful performance as a psychopathic hitman in Sam Peckinpah's *Bring Me the Head of Alfredo Garcia* (1975) seems horribly close to the real man, stripping away the veneer to reveal a tortured soul within. Watching Young in this bleak movie remains a disconcerting experience.

Irony strikes again with the title of his last film, *The Game of Death* (1979), a Bruce Lee martial arts extravaganza. During production in Hong Kong, Young met and married a gallery owner, Kim Schmidt, 33 years his junior.

Back in the United States it was a real game of death which Young was to play with Kim in their luxury duplex apartment opposite New York's Carnegie Hall. In what seems to have been a suicide pact, he shot his young wife and then shot himself. Police searching the apartment found a cache of revolvers and several hundred rounds of ammunition.

Where There's a Pill There's a Way

On the screen Alan Ladd was cool and unsmiling, moving from stone-faced calm to violent action like a hawser that suddenly snaps under pressure. Off the set, the pressure of being Alan Ladd – enduring the tired old jokes about his lack of height and limited range – finally shattered his brittle self-confidence. He once told a friend, 'I'm the most insecure guy in Hollywood.'

Disillusioned, he made a botched attempt to shoot himself in 1962. He was found at his ranch with gunshot wounds which were said to be accidental. Ladd was no stranger to suicide – in 1937 he had watched in horror as his mother, a hopeless alcoholic, died in convulsions after eating rat poison.

He tried again, in 1964, dosing himself with sedatives on top of alcohol. He didn't wake up. Ironically, his last, posthumous appearance was in *The Carpetbaggers* (1964), a rip-roaring tale of sex and skulduggery in Old Hollywood.

Sleeping pills, which had failed to waft Lupita Velez gracefully to the other side, were the chosen method of death for Charles Boyer, Gail Russell, Dorothy Dandridge, Carole Landis (distraught at being dumped by boyfriend Rex Harrison), Judy Garland (found crouched on the lavatory like a shrunken old crone), and most famously of all, Marilyn Monroe.

Marilyn had always been one of the most 'difficult' of stars, frequently unable to remember her lines, demanding take after take of the simplest scenes and almost always late on the set. During the shooting of her last film, John Huston's *The Misfits* (1961), co-starring Clark Gable and Montgomery Clift, she was a constant problem, and her regular fits of depression led to an overdose of sleeping pills.

Relations with her husband, the playwright Arthur Miller, had reached breaking point, and they were divorced only a week before the film's première. A terrible melancholy surrounds the movie: a few weeks after filming was completed, Clark Gable died of a heart attack caused by the strain of the location shooting; and Montgomery Clift died six years later, also from a heart attack, caused by heavy drinking.

Marilyn was not long for this world. Crack-up lay just around the corner. She began a new film, the ominously titled *Something's Got to Give*, but after an uninterrupted series of rows she was summarily dismissed. Deserted by her lovers, the last of whom was Robert Kennedy, she slipped her moorings and drifted away. On 5 August 1962 her nude body, an empty bottle of barbiturates beside it, was found by her housekeeper. Surviving fragments of *Something's Got to Give*, particularly a nude bathing scene, show that, even in extremis, she had lost none of her elusively luminous beauty that captivated the movie world.

Her story did not end there. Marilyn's death remains an enigma. The question of foul play has often been raised, but never conclusively proved. It was revealed that a secret diary had mysteriously vanished from her bedroom; allegedly, it contained information about her relations with the Kennedy brothers. A private eye claimed that she had been murdered by the CIA to prevent her from revealing a harebrained plot to assassinate the Cuban leader Fidel Castro. Others have suggested that she knew too much about the Mob's designs on the Kennedy brothers, which ultimately led to the assassination of President John F. Kennedy.

The endless flood of speculation and theory washes over her body, sprawled sadly in death. They won't stop pawing over Marilyn in death, just as they pawed over her in life. But the essential Marilyn remains with us on celluloid. Cameramen may often have cursed her, but the camera loved her till the end.

Hollywood Agonistes

Grisly self-willed ends litter the annals of Hollywood. Two-fisted half-Indian Art Accord, sagebrush hero of the silent screen, poisoned himself with cyanide when he failed to make the transition to sound. In 1931 make-up man George Westmore, one of a famous dynasty, ended it all in slow motion, downing a cocktail of biochloride of mercury which took four frightful days to sear its way through his innards. In 1935 actor Lou Tellegen committed hara-kiri with a pair of gold-plated scissors; he was found squatting naked on the floor, surrounded by blood-spattered piles of his old posters, stills and press clippings. Failed starlet Gwili Andre stepped into a similar pile of personal memorabilia, lit a match and burnt herself to a crisp.

James Whale, the homosexual British director of *Frankenstein* (1931) and *The Invisible Man* (1933), was an enigmatic figure, never at ease in Hollywood. By the 1950s he was a forgotten figure, consoling himself with his paintings, a succession of rent-boys and Havana cigars. Increasingly afflicted by illness, he went for his first and last swim in the pool by which he loved to lounge with his young lovers. His immaculately dressed body was found floating face down in the bright California sun, a scenario from one of his movies.

Accidents add to the catalogue of horror. Veteran actor Vic Morrow was sliced to shreds by the runaway rotor blade of a crashing helicopter during the filming of *The Twilight Zone* in 1981. In 1965 former Fox star Linda

Darnell – fat, 42 and finished – burnt to death in a friend's living room, where she had been watching one of her old films on TV. A dropped cigarette ignited her funeral pyre. Natalie Wood, on the comeback trail in 1982, went down for the third time in a drunken drowning accident. Ironically, she had always lived in fear of the sea.

The last word should be left to George Sanders, who for over 30 years padded down a path of silky villainy and purring caddishness, dispensing sneers and disdainful dialogue with the studied weariness of a man who has seen everything and is surprised by nothing. Nature created him to play Addison de Witt, the waspish theatre critic whose voice-over provides the barbed commentary to the backstage backstabbings in *All About Eve* (1950).

His performance in *All About Eve* won Sanders a Best Supporting Actor Oscar, but the success seemed to dismay the old cad into a long, slow decline. The voyage ended with a stint in drag in John Huston's *The Kremlin Letter* (1971) and as Beryl Reid's butler in *Psychomania* (1973), his last film. When it was released, he was already dead from a drugs overdose in a Spanish hotel. His suicide note blamed it all on boredom: 'Dear World: I am leaving you because I am bored. I am leaving you with your worries in this sweet cesspool.'

Addison de Witt would have no doubt arched a supercilious eyebrow at the news, but in truth it was rather sad.

Violin Cases and Hard Cash

Nowadays few Hollywood producers awake in the morning to find a sawn-off horse's head tucked under the duvet. In one of the most memorable, not to say startling, scenes from Francis Ford Coppola's *The Godfather* (1972), a Hollywood producer had refused to sign on a schmaltzy Italian tenor who was one of 'The Family' and so gained an unexpected bed-fellow as a result. Even though rumours that this resembled the way in which Frank Sinatra landed the part of Maggio in *From Here To Eternity* (1953) are probably completely untrue, this scenario jolted audiences into realizing the extent of the Mafia grip on movieland.

Willie the Pimp

It was actually a Chicago pimp, Willie Bioff, whose extra pounds were forced-fitted into expensively tailored suits, who started hustling local cinemas with such success that national Mafia muscle soon came flocking to him.

Bioff was only able to squeeze the studios until they bled cash and treat the moguls like serfs because the latter were aggressively anti-labour. Had the studio tyrants recognized workers' rights, which would have diminished the bitter and fraught struggle throughout the 1930s to create unions, then they would not have left the sizeable gap into which Bioff was able to jump.

The result was the IATSE scandal. The International Alliance of Theatrical State Employees was the union which represented the interests of gaffers,

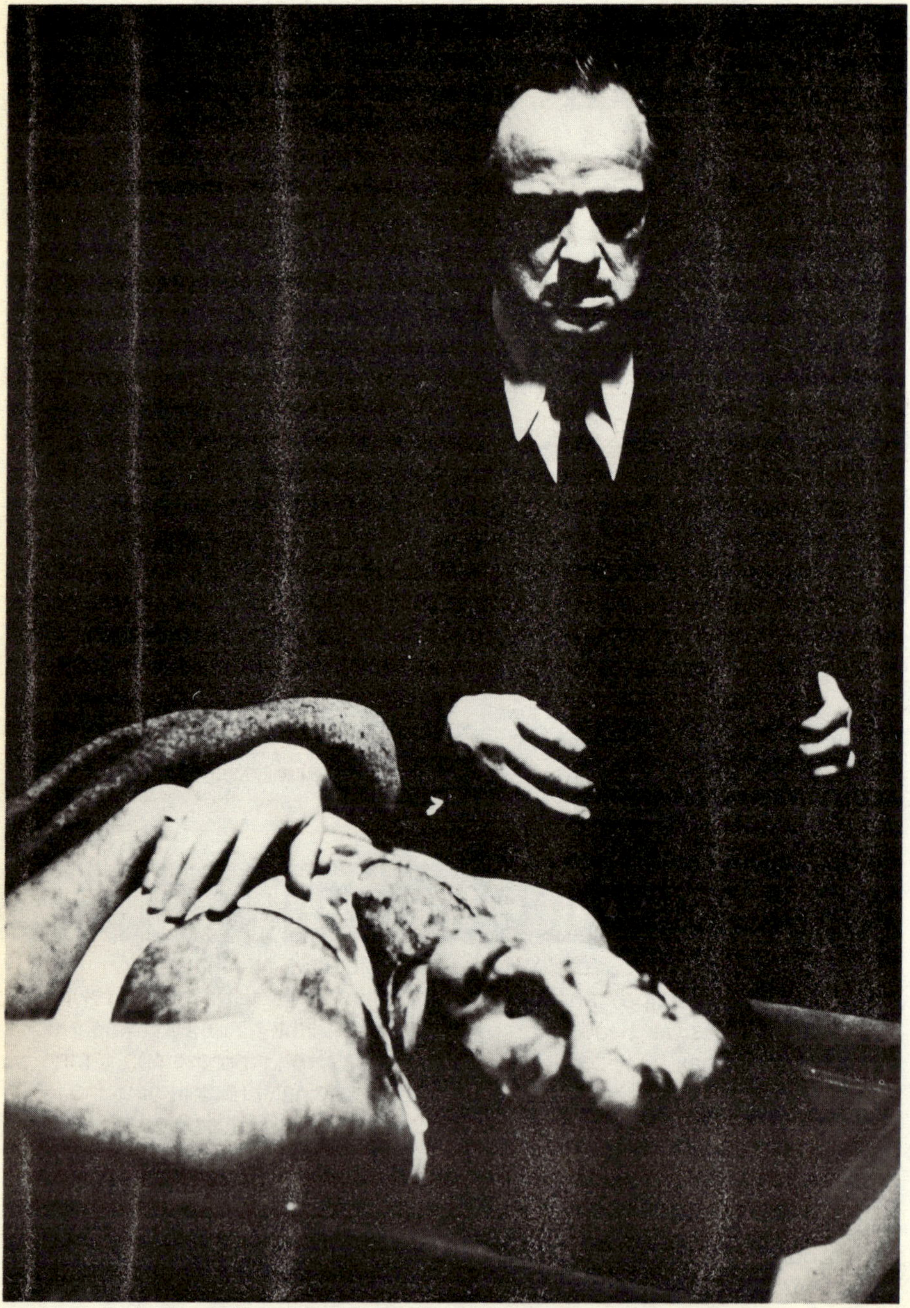

Scene from *The Godfather*, allegedly made with Mafia money!

grips, stagehands, make-up men, projectionists and art directors. With the help of George Browne, the new union president, Bioff was able to make the film industry his own.

The two creeps quickly applied relentless pressure on the Balaban and Katz cinema chain in Chicago. Balaban, who later became chairman of the board at Paramount, offered Browne $150 a week to forget about an agreement to expand the pay packets of cinema staff. Bioff sneered at this derisory two cents offer and blew a circuit, demanding in the process a one-off payment of $50,000. This was clearly an offer which Balaban felt he could refuse, so muscle moved in and a series of unfortunate 'accidents' were triggered at cinemas throughout the Balaban and Katz circuit. Films were screened backwards, *One Night of Love* (1934), a Grace Moore musical, was shown without music and a crucial and climactic motel scene in *It Happened One night* (1934) went strangely missing. How odd.

Audiences stormed out, demanding refunds, and newspapers were quick to brand Balaban as a cheap trickster. He almost ran to Bioff with the $50,000 and the two crooks were soon bragging about their easy pay. Enter big-time mobsters with bigger ideas.

'The Enforcer' himself, one Frank Nitti, was captivated by the fact that the two bully-boys had extorted a small fortune by *not* calling a projectionists' strike. An ally of Al Capone and with national ambitions of his own, he sent 'Cherry Nose' Gioe and well dressed associates, to announce that the Mob would receive half the proceeds from now on.

Lest there be any misunderstanding, two innocents were sprayed with bullets: T. E. Maloy, head of the projectionists' local 110, and Louis Alterie, president of the Janitors Union.

Now it was time for Bioff, Browne and their heavyweight partners to go truly national. Men who were destined to become legends of organized crime were called upon to lend their strength. Lepke Buchalter of Murder Incorporated, 'Lucky' Luciano and Paul 'The Waiter' Lucca joined hands with Frank Nitti to fix the election at the next IATSE convention in Louisville so that Browne would win the union presidency. Needless to say, he did. It may also be that Bioff's personal division of trigger-happy toughies, who had come all the way from Chicago especially for the occasion, helped win votes for Browne.

This same happy gang was soon to bring Hollywood a surprise treat. With Browne now living on the fringe as a figurehead president, the cumbersome task of extorting hard cash was left to Willie Bioff who quickly became chief 'businessman' for the entire syndicate. Running around Hollywood making film people offers they simply couldn't refuse, this oily little fattie not only 'advised' all wayward craftsmen of the advantages of joining IATSE but also squeezed the pips of the moguls. As quick as you could shout 'Action!', he reduced their bank balances lest they be confronted by the unhappy coincidence of projectionists' strikes from coast to coast.

Within a short time the two Chicago hustlers were also operating on the east coast. One of their first appointments in New York was with Nick Schenck, president of Loew's Inc. which ran MGM from New York City. Schenck was outraged at their demand for $2 million and just couldn't believe that two street-smarts possessed enough clout to lock a big picture corporation in a vice. He was to learn. After deciding with Sidney Kent, president of 20th Century-Fox, to poke the hoods in the eye, they were immediately 'given to understand' that the two B's could switch off every studio light in Hollywood with a mere phone call. Like two meek schoolboys Schenck and Kent went to see Bioff in his room at the Warwick Hotel, Schenck offering up his contribution in a brown paper bag.

Even the malevolent despots were forced to buckle under. Once when Bioff refused to deal with Paramount, the studio head went running to placate him like a sycophantic errand boy; on another, Jack Warner was ordered by Bioff to come down and personally welcome him at the gates when he had difficulty gaining entry without a pass.

Only Sam Goldwyn tried to withstand Bioff's bullying for a while. An unintentional purveyor of malapropisms, he came out with a line which is remembered to this day. At a meeting of the Motion Picture Producers and Directors of America, which was in session to discuss negotiating terms with Bioff, Sam stood up and, reaching for his hat, said, 'Gentlemen, include me out.'

Bioff manipulated his shrewdness to exploit every corner of the movie business. He generously offered himself to MGM, Fox and Warners as their 'agent' for purchasing film stock. Receiving a handy 7 per cent for his tireless efforts, he naturally had absolutely no resistance from Jules Brulator, who distributed Eastman film stock in Hollywood. Brulator knew the result of unhappy business arrangements with bully-boy Bioff. With the film stock operation brought to heel, Bioff enriched the syndicate by more than $150,000 per year. He was equally considerate to the members of the union he ran. In return for vast sums, he kindly agreed to trample on any wage claims by the members while he simultaneously upped the annual membership fee. As usual his entrepreneurial successes were split between himself and the syndicate.

However, one brave man drove in a thick wedge which eventually put paid to Bioff's reign of terror. The tough old editor of *Daily Variety* was Arthur Ungar whose honesty shone bright in a town where morals had been bought off by movies. Disgusted by the plethora of grubby scams with which Bioff had coated Hollywood, honest Arthur decided to wage war in print.

Robert Montgomery, president of

the Screen Actors Guild, was quick to come to his aid. Horrified at Bioff's pushy attempts to sink his teeth into the Guild, he commissioned a private detective to dig up some juicy facts from Bioff's own crummy past. His sentence for pimping back in Chicago quickly rose to the surface and Ungar was only too happy to splash all the details across the pages of *Daily Variety*.

Both men enthused Westbrook Pegler in the wake of their revelations. Pegler, a high-profile columnist who was syndicated across the country, dented Bioff's credibility even further by printing a series of savoury stories on the gangster.

But it was the plodding old tax inspectors who finally dumped on Bioff. They informed the government, which by now was keen to see Bioff behind bars, about the presence of a cheque for $100,000 which Bioff had received from Joseph M. Schenck, chairman of 20th Century-Fox, president of the Motion Picture Producers Association, and producer of most of Buster Keaton's silent films.

Insisting that the fat fee was only intended as a loan, Schenck was cornered into admitting that it was in fact a large pay-off. He was convicted of perjury, given a year in prison and lost his citizenship. However, his sizeable contributions to Democratic Party funds over the years were not overlooked by President Truman, who pardoned Schenck, restored his citizenship and left him free to return to Fox as an executive producer.

One studio boss now followed another in confessing to the creative accounting so necessary to meet Bioff's grasping demands. Both Bioff and Browne at last stood trial before a federal grand jury in New York on 23 May 1941 and were nailed for squeezing financial goodies from Fox, MGM, Warner Brothers and Paramount. In return for their exhaustive efforts, Browne went down for eight years, while Bioff was packed off to Alcatraz for ten.

A true gent to the last, Bioff talked non-stop once inside. He trotted out the names of the seven Chicago hoodlums who had engineered this takeover of Hollywood. Frank Nitti, Al Capone's previous enforcer, shot himself through the head in a Chicago railway yard on hearing the good news.

After Alcatraz Bioff went to live in Phoenix, Arizona, where he called himself Willie Nelson, investor. On 4 November 1955, he was going to pop into town to check on his shares. He stepped into his car, turned the key and was promptly blown to bits. Unsurprisingly, the police were not at great pains to discover who had put an end to the man who brought the Mafia to Hollywood.

And so the steamroller tactics of mob rule ensured that movieland was like plasticine in the hands of a happy, gurgling infant. It was widely considered that even at this early stage Bioff and his antics had claimed the Attorney General and even punctured the White House itself.

'The Joker is Wild'

In the wake of this, Hollywood set about cleaning up its films about the Chicago Mob from which it now strained (on screen) to keep a puritanical distance. Good old Frank Sinatra, about whom more scurrilous speculation regarding Mafia links has been made than any other entertainer, played the part of Joe E. Lewis in *The Joker is Wild* (1957). Predictably Hollywood reduced the hoods in the film to the level of cartoon wise-guys. In reality, Lewis was a singer-comedian whose throat had been slashed for his unfortunate refusal to tread the boards of a Mafia nightclub. 'Machine Gun' Jack McGurn was the nastie with the knife on whom history was to pile the telling evidence that he masterminded the St Valentine's Day Massacre. In the film the studio conversion kit turns the hit-man into a yapping wisecracker who would be a more suitable match for Bugs Bunny.

McGurn's loyal tribe, who were left intact when 'Machine Gun' was blown off the streets in 1936, were the most influential mobsters in the States when Sinatra made the movie. Chief Mafioso was Sam Giancana, once a gunslinger for Al Capone, who took over the Chicago outfit in 1959. A tough-nosed operator, he was quick to boost the Mob's already massive income from Hollywood and Las Vegas. With his celebrity chums, and especially his long-term shenanigans with singer Phyllis McGuire, it comes as no surprise at all that his daughter, Antoinnette, craved a life in the spotlight. Dad immediately fixed a top-level meeting for her at MGM.

She has been quite open about her father's grip on the studios: 'If Sam wanted to send his little girl to Hollywood, or if he just wanted a friend to play a movie role, or if he just wanted to see the studio sights and meet some stars, he got what he wanted, and he got it with red carpet treatment.'

Hollywood has yet to make a movie about its own seedy partnership with the Mafia. Applauded at the time for its unzipping of hoodlum rule on the Brooklyn shore in *On The Waterfront* (1954), it would never have had the gall to turn Brando into Bioff and so detail the gift-wrapped package which it had already been delivering to the Mafia for years.

The almost invisible line between the Mob and the moguls is further blurred when one considers the links between actors and hoods. Jean Harlow had a long-term relationship with Longie Zwillman, the New Jersey prohibition king, while George Raft spent all his time as a boy on the streets of New York with all kinds of toughies, some of whom later took centre-stage as star gangsters. One of Raft's boyhood buddies was Bugsy Siegel, the bootlegger and chief hit-man for Murder Inc., who improved his career credits when he turned acres of sand

Frank Sinatra and Jeanne Crain in scene from *The Joker is Wild*.

into Las Vegas and so thoughtfully created a limitless new cash flow for the 'Families'.

As Raft's star faded from sight, he was happy to accept work which was sought out for him by both Siegel and Mayer Lansky, the financial whizz of the entire syndicate.

Even today the links persist. James Caan, who in *The Godfather* played the hot-headed Sonny whose life is ended by rival bullets at a New Jersey toll booth, seemed to step straight off the set when he appeared in court to defend an 'old friend', Andrew Russo. Recently released from a five-year jail term for bribery and tax evasion, he was now taking the stand for bribery and extortion. Considered by the FBI to be a high-flying member of the Colombo family (one of New York's top five), he was extolled by Caan who came out with the classic cliché: 'I don't know if there is a Mafia.' The prosecutor, Rudolph Giuliani, was amazed that Caan could even speak because, as he said, 'I thought he was killed at the toll booth.'

Caan seemed also to be intimately acquainted with Mafia protocol. Loyally providing verbal support for Russo's chum, Carmine 'The Shake' Persico (the Colombo family boss), he kissed Persico, Brando-style, on the cheek.

Caan and Russo seem to have become friends during the shooting of *The Godfather*. At that time Joe Colombo was still running his own family. As a ruse to lessen the pressure from the FBI flatfoots, he founded the Italian American Civil Rights League which began to claim that 'Mafia' was a term of racial abuse which the FBI, not to mention the Italian-haters amongst the WASP establishment, was guilty of spreading willy-nilly. This led to a veto on the terms 'Mafia' and 'Cosa Nostra' in not only all FBI public statements but also in *The Godfather* itself.

The Peraino offshoot of the Colombo clan was not content with just shaping films but wanted to actually make them. Louis 'Butcher' Peraino and a former Brooklyn barber, Gerald Damiano, were the puppeteers behind *Deep Throat* (1972) and its star Linda Lovelace. After dropping $22,000 into the pot, the final reward for the Colombos was around $100m. Peraino and his brother Joseph soon sank their teeth into Hollywood with tasteful excursions which included *The Devil in Miss Jones* (1973), *Andy Warhol's Frankenstein* (1974), *Return of the Dragon* (1973) (starring Bruce Lee) and the enormous cash-creator, *Texas Chainsaw Massacre* (1975). One producer even told the *Los Angeles Times* that, when you dealt with the brothers, you never knew whether you were negotiating for your picture or your life.

Francis Ford Coppola, director of *The Godfather*, was again blessed with Mafia involvement in *The Cotton Club* (1984). The money-men who funded the picture were Ed and Fred Doumani, who still own the El Morocco casino in Las Vegas, a joint which has hosted visits-a-plenty from FBI investigators who have the nasty guff of gangland connections in their nostrils.

When the film's budget disappeared off the graph, soaring from $20 million to $47 million, the brothers sent a 'good friend' to teach Coppola basic book-keeping. Joey Cusumano arrived as the producer and, unsurprisingly, the high-spending director finished filming before the deadline. Still, Cusumano, who was followed for six months by two FBI cars for 24 hours a day, couldn't return the $27 million which has left a gaping hole in the Doumanis' pocket.

The Doumanis, of course, kept their distance from the film set by staying in Las Vegas. They epitomize the new era of sleek mobsters who do not run around like Bioff emptying gun barrels at those who transgress. Instead they employ smooth-talking puppets as respectable fronts for their operations. Even today, if you want to make a trouble-free movie, you have to be able to negotiate the complex path which eventually leads back to the Mob. Willie Bioff would approve.

Malice in Wonderland

Hedda and Louella – Hollywood's Harpies

Tittle-tattle, innuendo, downright lies and, from time to time, the awful truth – these were the principal ingredients of the bubbling witches' brew which was ladelled out in the Hollywood gossip columns. Who was screwing who? Who was divorcing who? Who was falling apart at the seams? Who was a crypto-Commie, ripe for public exposure? Who cared if today's lead story was a mess of garbled rubbish? You could always print an apology tomorrow.

Hubble bubble, toil and trouble. For 40 years the gossip columns' principal toiler, troublemaker and harridan-in-chief was Louella Parsons. Lumpen, lard-faced Louella virtually invented this journalistic sub-species. She had a head start. In 1924 she became motion picture editor of the *New York American*, owned by William Randolph Hearst, a newspaper baron whose methods make Rupert Murdoch look like a Boy Scout, and a man who was never overly concerned with the true facts if they got in the way of the 'Big Story'.

That year Hearst's mistress, film star Marion Davies, invited Louella out to California. When she arrived in Hollywood, it took the ferociously ambitious Louella about two minutes to realize that here was the honey pot around which she could buzz and sting most effectively. Insider knowledge, and the backing of the mighty Hearst chain, were to provide a route to wealth and remarkable power over the film capital's élite.

Ironically, Louella was the

Many a Hollywood star's bane, gossip magazine *Confidential*.

archetypal outsider. She was no glamour puss. Even in her days of glory Louella looked like everyone's frumpish maiden aunt from Moose Droppings, Idaho. But like the millions of Mid-Western nobodies who read her column, she was a true fan and a passionate believer in the mink-packaged fantasy of Hollywood peddled by the studios' publicity machines. For movie-struck Louella the tinsel on the inside was every bit as real as the tinsel on the outside. But there were other things on the inside, lurking just below the glittering surface: adultery, addiction, mental breakdown and a host of peccadilloes which might destroy a career overnight. Therein lay the secret of Louella's power. It was the stories she did not print which gave her a vice-like grip on the studios and the stars.

In his autobiography, *Bring on the Empty Horses*, David Niven painted an imaginary but all-too-real picture of the machinations which Louella used to get her exclusives:

> COLUMNIST: Who was that girl you were nuzzling in that little bar in the San Fernando Valley at three o'clock this morning?
> ACTOR: I was with my mother.
> COLUMNIST: According to my information, you had one of her bosoms in your hand.
> ACTOR: It fell out of her dress. . . I was just helping her put it back in.
> COLUMNIST: Rubbish!. . . But I won't print it because I don't want to make trouble for you.
> ACTOR: Bless you – you're a doll.
> COLUMNIST: Got any news for me?
> ACTOR: Afraid I haven't right now.
> COLUMNIST: Call me when you hear anything, dear.
> ACTOR: (wiping his brow) You bet I will.

And he would, too.

Louella's column was forever in the throes of terminal dyslexia. Accuracy, and anything resembling correct spelling and syntax, were regularly forgotten in the avalanche of mangled gush extruded by the fearless journalist. Her keen sense of priorities was revealed in the famous lines she wrote in April 1939, after the Italian invasion of Albania: 'The deadly dullness of last week was lifted today when Darryl Zanuck admitted that he had bought the rights to Maurice Maeterlinck's *The Bluebird*.'

Her tastelessness knew no bounds. She once interrupted the soap opera she hosted, 'Hollywood Hotel', to inform the audience in her high nasal whine, 'Friends, I want to tell you that Lowell Sherman died just a few moments ago.'

Occasionally, she hit the bull's-eye. When Mae West arrived in Hollywood, Louella observed of that matchlessly pneumatic and ageless star, 'The buxom, blonde Mae West, fat, fair and I don't know how near forty.' Later West was to claim that Louella had become a good friend; this was the most prudent way to treat the old baggage. Dealing with Louella was rather like handling a bad-tempered rattlesnake – and a rattlesnake with a taste for blackmail.

The stars and the studios hedged their bets with expensive gifts. One Christmas Carole Lombard presented Louella with a mirrored bathroom, conjuring up a grisly vision of multiple images of the flabby old hag competing with each other as she went about her ablutions. When she married for the second time, the studios presented the happy couple with gifts worth $250,000.

Louella's second husband was Dr Harry Martin, universally known as 'Docky' and a character as absurd as his simpering spouse. Allegedly, 'Docky' had been a brilliant medical student, but by the time he became Hollywood's premier 'clap doctor' he was a man with a great future behind him. When Louella met 'Docky' he was the house doctor to Lee Frances, who ran the film capital's choicest bordello.

A hopeless alcoholic, 'Docky' was usually incapable after a couple of snorts. On one famous occasion when her husband passed out at a party Louella's reaction was both protective and practical: 'Don't disturb him – he has to operate tomorrow.' An apocryphal version of the story has 'Docky' in fancy dress, a billowing Roman toga, whose folds fell apart to reveal his member. A passing wag quipped, 'Look, there's Louella's column.'

'Docky's medical contacts provided Louella with a hotline to some of Hollywood's most intimate secrets. Rarely did she fail to scoop the field with news of a star's pregnancy, often before the mother-to-be's rabbit test results had been passed on to her doctor. Lab assistants were only one strand in Louella's intelligence web, which included switchboard operators, the staff at beauty parlours, janitors, doormen and florists. Louella could ring straight through to Louis B. Mayer or Jack Warner any time she wanted, but some of her hottest tips came from discreetly anonymous sources. A star could not send a bunch of flowers to his mistress without considering the possibility that the florist might dial Louella the moment he left the shop.

Like all second-raters, Louella reserved her deepest contempt for the truly first-rate, not least of them the boy-wonder Orson Welles. His *Citizen Kane* (1941) was a thinly disguised portrait of William Randolph Hearst, although the passage of time has, with great poignancy, turned the film into a portrait of Welles' own rise and fall. When Louella got wind of what was afoot, the Hearst newspaper chain declared war on Welles' studio, RKO, which was in severe financial difficulties at the time.

Foolishly, RKO had tried to keep Louella away from a press showing of *Citizen Kane*. This was no better than pouring oil on the flames, which by now were threatening to engulf the film. At one point RKO considered recouping their money by selling the print to a consortium of studios, who would then have destroyed it. That one of the milestones of cinema could have been threatened with casual incineration is testimony to the malign power wielded by Louella and the organization she represented.

Hearst newspapers successfully disrupted the release of *Citizen Kane*, and it was years before it was recognized as a masterpiece. Louella never forgave Welles. No mention of his name was included in her column unless it was attached to a derogatory item.

Here Comes Hedda

By the early 1940s, Louella had a rival, Hedda Hopper, charitably described by Ray Milland as 'an unmitigated bitch . . . . venomous, vicious, a pathological liar and quite stupid'.

Hedda was nudging 50 before she hit the big-time. In the mid-1930s she was just another general-purpose actress whose career was going nowhere. Ironically, Louella had been one of her early boosters in the silent days, dubbing her the 'Queen of the Quickies'. Now she was living on her wits and her friendship with MGM screenwriter Frances Marion and Louella's old chum Marion Davies. It was Davies who gave Hedda her start in journalism in 1935, writing a weekly fashion column in *The Washington Post*.

Initially Louella continued to root for Hedda, but in 1939 they had become deadly rivals. 'Hedda Hopper's Hollywood', syndicated by Esquire Features, was appearing in the *Los Angeles Times*, the *New York Daily News* and *The Chicago Tribune*. For the first time Louella had a serious competitor, a development which was welcomed by the studios. The gloves came off and a battle was joined which lasted for 20 years. Frequently the stars were caught in the crossfire. If one of them favoured Louella with a juicy morsel, he would quickly find himself the object of one of Hedda's vendettas. And vice versa.

Louella always affected a flutteringly vague manner which, until her later failing years, concealed a mind like a bear trap. Hedda adopted a brasher approach. She revelled in pointing dramatically at her home on Tropical Drive in Beverly Hills and chortling, 'That's the home fear built!'

Like Louella, Hedda had only the haziest grasp of what real journalism was about. Sometimes this could be almost endearing. Ringing the *Los Angeles Times* with a scoop, she shrieked down the line, 'Stop the presses – whatever that means!'

She started as she meant to go on. In her very first column she reported that Greta Garbo, who was soon to marry Leopold Stokowski, had undergone inspection by the famous conductor's patrician Philadelphia parents. Not only did the romance prove to be non-existent, but so did the Philadelphia relatives. This rivalled the immortal story filed by Louella that Sigmund Freud was going to be hired by Warners to act as the technical adviser on the Bette Davis weepie, *Now Voyager* (1942). Presumably Jack Warner had paranormal powers, as Siggy was busy being dead at the time.

All too rarely did Hedda's carelessness with these awkward little facts catch up with her. When she refused to stop running a story that Joseph Cotten was having an extra-marital affair with Deanna Durbin, Cotten took his revenge. Espying the statuesque Hopper at a party, he promptly planted a hefty kick in the middle of her fat backside. On another occasion Ann Sheridan, taxed beyond endurance, dumped a plate of mashed potato in her lap.

Hedda never forgot or forgave the slights and petty humiliations she had endured in her days as a humble supporting actress! Years before, she had been snubbed on the set by Joan Bennett. When Bennett's husband, producer Walter Wanger, shot her lover, the agent Jennings Lang, in the groin, Hedda had a field day, wallowing in righteous indignation. Joan Bennett responded by sending Hedda a unique Valentine – a skunk – with the accompanying note:

Here's a little Valentine
That very plainly tells
The reason it reminded me so much of you –
It smells!

However, the majority of stars were happy to lick her boots, as is evidenced by this fawning telegram signed by Gary Cooper, William (Hopalong Cassidy) Boyd, John Wayne, Harry Carey and Roy Rogers:

HEDDA YOU OLD HOPTOAD. FIRST YOU WENT TO TEXAS. NOW YOU'RE IN ARIZONA. THAT'S COW COUNTRY AND THAT MEANS COWBOYS. AND COWBOYS MEANS LOTS OF FUN FOR ALL AMERICA. SO HAVE A GOOD TIME. BUT FOR GOSH SAKES DON'T FORGET TO COME BACK TO US. REGARDS AND SUCCESS FROM THE 'ARIZONA GANG'.

Presumably the reference to 'cow country' was merely a Freudian slip.

According to one story, Merle Oberon, reeling from Hedda's attacks, took her out to lunch at the Vine Street Derby. When Merle asked what had caused this tidal wave of bile, Hedda replied exultantly, 'Nothing, dear. It's bitchery. Sheer bitchery.'

Hedda reserved her most pungent bitchery for Louella. On one famous occasion they both attended a show staged at Hollywood's Moulin Rouge for opera star Helen Traubel. In the finale a small flock of doves was released. They were supposed to settle tastefully on the girls of the chorus line but, distracted by the lights and music, they flew about the auditorium in confusion. As the feathers began to drift down on to the audience, Hedda leapt to her feet, hissing, 'Let's get out of here! Those birds are going to shit! And when they do, I hope they hit Louella's bald spot!'

The shit certainly hit the fan when, in her autobiography, *The Whole Truth and Nothing But*, Hedda claimed that she had tried to dissuade Elizabeth Taylor from marrying Michael Wilding because he had had a homosexual relationship with Stewart Granger. Straight back zinged a libel suit for $3,000,000. The book was closed with a substantial out-of-court settlement and a full apology from Hedda.

In a world in which everyone was either on the way up or on the way down, this pair of carrion crows clung to their perches for nearly 20 years. In part their success lay in their crude but instinctive feel for public opinion. Hedda and Louella were never ones to swim against the tide. They were seldom, if ever, the first to break the real Hollywood tragedies, like Frances Farmer's mental collapse. In cases like these, they were content to trot along in the rear, happy to put the stiletto heel into a woman who was already down.

Ultimately, they were the studios' creatures, and in their coy references to sex (for which read 'dating') or heavy drinking (for which read remarks like, 'Aren't all those late-night revels taking their toll on Constance Bennett's beauty?') they acted as apologists for the erratic antics of the stars. For all their power, they never pushed their luck too far.

As Louella frequently observed in her column, 'Tempus sure does fugit!' It made them old and confused, struggling to survive in a world which had left them, and the studio system on which they fed, far behind. David Niven once remarked that Hedda and Louella had skins as tough as a brontosaurus. Now they *were* brontosauri, near-extinct dinosaurs, grazing fretfully on increasingly meagre pastures.

As she became increasingly doddery, Louella relied almost exclusively on studio hand-outs to fill her column. She would drift through film-land parties, stuffing them abstractedly into an enormous handbag. At one party she was approached by a young gatecrasher proffering a hand-out on which several stars had already signed their autographs. Not realizing that she, too, was being asked to sign, she shot out her claw and crammed the crumpled paper into her bag. Later, in her office, an assistant found her gazing tearfully at it and wailing, 'What are they trying to tell me?' The message, Louella, was: 'You're all washed up!'

Hedda finally succumbed to double pneumonia in 1966. Louella outlasted her rival by six years, ending her days in a nursing home where she sat mute before the television, bathed in the ghostly glow of the stars she had alternately fawned upon and terrorized.

Strictly Confidential

In the 1950s there was one magazine which was happy to 'boldly go' where Hedda and Louella prudently feared to tread – *Confidential*, the sleaze sheet owned by Robert Harrison.

Confidential appeared in 1952, at a

time when the power of the major studios was on the wane. In their heyday, the heads of studios were the first to be called if a star wandered on to the wrong side of the law. MGM's Louis B. Mayer arrived at the scene of the suicide of Jean Harlow's husband, Paul Bern, a full two hours before the boys in blue. Significantly, it was Mayer who handed over the suicide note allegedly written by Bern, and who ensured that the tricky questions raised by the coroner's inquest were suppressed. He was protecting his investment. But times were changing, and many of the stars were now freelancers who could no longer rely on the old-time studio empires, with their almost limitless resources, to protect them.

Into this squalid arena oozed slimeball Harrison, a former porn-merchant who had cut his journalistic teeth on a legendary scandal sheet, the *Daily GraphiC*. Harrison based his editorial approach on the bullying tactics adopted by the House Un-American Activities Committee (HUAC) investigators in the Communist witch-hunts of the late 1940s and early 1950s. Innuendo and guilt by association were the order of the day. Truth was usually tossed out of the window.

Confidential's motto was: 'Tells the Facts and Names the Names'. Its style was a mixture of *Police Gazette* and Mickey Spillane on speed. Its formula was simple: an unflattering candid shot of a star and then a story alleging homosexuality, misogyny, drunkenness or vicious domestic strife.

And those were the flattering profiles! How about some samples?

LIZABETH SCOTT IN THE CALL GIRL'S CALL BOOK

Just a roving check ma'am and out popped. . . The vice cops expected to find a few big name customers when they grabbed the date book of a trio of Hollywood Jezebels, but even their cast-iron nerves got a jolt when they got to the S's! In recent years Scotty's almost nonexistent career has allowed her to roam farther afield. In one jaunt to Europe she headed straight for Paris and the left bank where she took up with Frede, the city's most notorious lesbian queen and operator of a nightclub devoted exclusively to entertaining deviates just like herself!

Or:

KIM NOVAK AND SAMMY DAVIS JR

Who broke up their romance?

Exclusive! Boy meets girl, boy gets girl. . . It's a Hollywood movie plot no more. Here's how Hollywood broke Sammy's spirit on the rocks. It's the tragic love story of the century. In Romeo and Juliet the lovers could only be reunited in death . . . when their parents wouldn't let them marry. In real life a king gives up his throne for the woman he loves and gives up a $5 million bank account. In this case SAMMY DAVIS JR WOULDN'T GIVE UP THE NEGRO RACE! Kim Novak wouldn't give up the white race! Of course, there was the fact that his skin was black and her skin was white, but in Hollywood there's no such thing as a color line.

Harry Cohn, the volatile head of Columbia, took Sammy aside and said, 'Do you realize this girl is worth $20 million to me? Have a fling for a few months, but don't get married.' A dramatic decision had to be made. . . Sammy made it. He married a colored girl. Maybe his marriage had something to do with the visit Sammy received from two of Cohn's thugs, who said to Sammy, 'YOU HAVE ONE EYE NOW. WANT TO TRY FOR NONE? WELL THAT'S THE WAY THE FUTURE LOOKS IF YOU DON'T MARRY A COLORED GIRL WITHIN THREE DAYS OR ELSE!' A few months later Cohn himself was dead. Rumors going around Columbia said that [Kim and Sammy's] romance had killed Harry.

Harrison's informants were a motley crew of high-class hookers, out-of-work actors and washed-up journalists. Sometimes Hollywood's élite informed on each other. The Harry Cohn story was supplied by producer Mike Todd, a man only marginally less of a demented egomaniac than the beast of the Columbia lot. Stories were also fed to *Confidential* by two New York-based 'luminaries' of the gossip-column, the odious Walter Winchell and his rival Lee Mortimer. Winchell even plugged the magazine on television.

Infra-red, ultra-rapid film and high-powered telephoto lenses were some of the paparazzi techniques used by *Confidential* to pry into the private lives of the stars. In this way it acquired intimate pictures of a domestic slugfest between British actor Anthony Steel and his busty wife Anita Ekberg.

It was with this kind of 'research' that Harrison blackmailed the stars. Many paid up to avoid being splashed across the pages of *Confidential* in exposés like: *Dan Dailey in Drag*; *PSSST! Vic Mature: That Cute Trick You dated? 'She' was a 'HE'*; *Errol Flynn and His Two-Way Mirrors*; *The Best Pumper in Hollywood? M-M-M-Marilyn M-M-M-Monroe*; and an old chestnut, *Rory Calhoun – But for the Grace of God Still a Convict!*

Eventually the worms began to turn. The day after *Confidential* had featured a compromising item about Grace Kelly, her father burst into Harrison's New York office, smashed up his desk and poked the fearless publisher on the jaw. Early in 1957 Dorothy Dandridge, the black star of *Carmen Jones* (1954), filed a $2 million suit against *Confidential* after it had printed a feature on her allegedly naked cavortings in the woods with a bunch of fun-loving 'naturists'.

The floodgates were opened, and the stars began to line up to take legal potshots at their tormentor. Immediately alarm bells began ringing in the studios. If the stars were to take the stand, heaven knows what embarrassing revelations some smart-ass attorney might coax out of them. Once again it was cover-up time. When they failed to persuade California's Attorney-General to kill the actions against *Confidential* (by the subtle method of threatening to withdraw the industry's financial support for the Republican Party) the studios ensured that all the stars were as far away as possible, 'on holiday', when the proceedings began.

There were only two exceptions: Dandridge, who withdrew her complaint after a considerable out-of-court settlement; and fiery red-headed, green-eyed Irish-born star Maureen O'Hara, who was holding out for damages of $5,000,000.

Confidential had run a story in which it alleged that O'Hara played a game of 'Chinese Chest' in the loge section of Grauman's Chinese Theater with a South American gigolo. *Confidential* told its readers: 'The couple saw a couple who heated up the balcony as if it was July. Maureen, blouse unbuttoned and her hair in disarray, had assumed, in order to watch the movie, the oddest posture ever to be beheld in the entire history of motion pictures. She was stretched out on three seats, the lucky South American occupying the middle chair, while a picture denouncing juvenile delinquency was shown on the screen.'

The judge, obviously a man with a sense of humour, decided to re-enact the sordid scene *in situ*. The manager of Grauman's played Maureen's lucky Latin lover, and a reporter stood in for the tawny-haired star, raising her legs in the air for the edification of the jury. The seats were then minutely examined.

After these surreal solemnities, real-life took over. On 16 August one of *Confidential*'s editors, Polly Gould, committed suicide. She had been due to take the stand the following day. Her death was not unconnected with the fact that she had been playing both ends against the middle – acting as a stoolie for the DA and keeping Harrison informed of impending legal moves against him.

On the 17th O'Hara made her first appearance in court, brandishing a passport which seemed to prove that she had been in Spain at the time of the back-seat canoodling. But the witnesses would not be budged. Maureen's sister, an Irish nun, took the stand to vouch for the star's spotless character. There was even a lie detector test which proved inconclusive.

Eventually *Confidential* was ordered to pay $5,000 damages. Cheap at the price, perhaps, but only the first of a series of much more expensive settlements with a dozen stars. Liberace, for example, took the magazine for $40,000.

Shortly afterwards, Harrison's editor-in-chief, the rabid Red-baiting Howard Rushmore, shot and killed his wife while riding in a cab in New York's Upper East Side and then turned the gun on himself. Harrison sold *Confidential* and launched a new scandal sheet, *Inside News*. But his days were numbered. There was now pap aplenty for the public pouring from their television screens. And the stars were revealing all in 'fuck and tell' autobiographies like Errol Flynn's *My Wicked, Wicked Ways*, which was published in 1957. *Confidential*'s reign of terror was over.

However, its spirit lives on. Doesn't *Confidential*'s parade of outrageous fabrications, its prurience, homophobia and total absence of any journalistic standards have a depressingly familiar ring? Yes, *Confidential* is alive and well, flourishing in the boob-splattered pages of Britain's tabloid press.

FEUDIN', FUSSIN'

In its heyday, Hollywood was the world's most glamorous company town. But behind the glittering façade it was as volatile as any of its roughneck mining counterparts far from civilization. Even in Hollywood the fists, fur and feathers flew with monotonous regularity, the inevitable result of a heady cocktail of monstrously oversized egos, tiny minds and far, far too much alcohol (and often drugs).

The kingdom of conspicuous consumption was also noted for conspicuous public punch-ups between conspicuously public people. So much so that in the autumn of 1944 Herman Hover, the proprietor of one of Hollywood's most popular watering holes, Ciro's, announced his intention of installing a boxing ring in his club, to accommodate the brawlers who were using the dance floor for fisticuffs rather than the Rhumba.

AND A-FIGHTIN'

Hollywood Slugfests

The Cocoanut Grove – opened in 1921 and decorated with a small forest of fake palm trees salvaged from the set of *The Sheik* – was one of Hollywood's most famous nightspots. It was also famous for its fights. One of the most memorable broke out at an MGM party given for one of Louis B. Mayer's studio herd riders, the ex-bouncer Eddie Mannix. At the height of the party the drunken Mannix stumbled on to the bandstand and pushed aside the drummer in Gus Arnheim's orchestra. The subsequent machine-gun bursts of crazed thrashing stretched the patience of a Warners contingent, led by screenwriter Wilson Mizner, to breaking point and beyond. When Mannix refused to give way, a free-for-all erupted in which the MGM and Warners men traded punches on the dance floor like ice hockey players in a melee. Mizner – reputedly the model for the character Clark Gable played in *San Francisco* (1936) – laid Mannix out cold, launching him on a triple somersault before he came to rest.

On one exciting night in 1944, Hollywood's niteries seemed to be in a state of spontaneous combustion. At Romanoff's restaurant the owner, 'Prince' Michael Romanoff, was scrapping with racing car driver Barney Oldfield; at the Somerset House restaurant rugged Charles Bickford took exception to some 'unpatriotic' remarks made by a couple of strangers and waded in, fists flying; and over at bandleader Tommy Dorsey's Sunset Plaza home a small war broke out involving Dorsey and his wife, actors Jon Hall, Edward Norris and Antonio Icaza, and Winston Churchill's third cousin Jane. Broken beer bottles, carving knifes, the Los Angeles DA and the FBI eventually figured in this cheerful fracas, which was apparently triggered off when Jon Hall gave Mrs Dorsey 'a supposedly friendly pat on the backside'.

Hollywood women too were noted scrappers, and there were few if any who could stay the distance with Mexican Spitfire Lupe Velez. In his *Memoirs of a Hollywood Prince*, Budd Schulberg left an indelible picture of the little termagent: 'How many times had we seen the tempestuous Lupe in the front row at the Hollywood Legion stadium, pounding on the blood-stained canvas of the ring and screaming profane Mexican incantations at brown-skinned countrymen who were failing to live up to her high standards of combat? One night we had seen her stand up and cup her hands to shout some words of pugilistic wisdom to a handsome Mexican-Indian lightweight named Rojas. Rojas turned to look at Lupe. Lupe was easy to look at. In fact he had been openly flirting with her between rounds. Even I, who professed to hate girls, and who was surrounded by young women whose

profession it was to be pretty, found myself staring at Lupe. So Rojas turned his head and looked down the better to hear Lupe's advice. It was the last thing he heard for several minutes as he lay unconscious on the canvas, his head so close to Lupe's that she could have reached out and cradled

George Raft and Edward G. Robinson fought for Marlene Dietrich's attention.

her fallen gladiator in her arms. Instead she was screaming, "HIJO! Get up, you son-of-a-beech. . . !"'

Lupe needed no encouragement to clamber into the ring herself. At Ciro's one night, her husband Johnny Weissmuller was being needled by an overly aggressive customer. Johnny, a gentle soul at heart, was tactfully trying to extricate himself without trouble when Lupe dived in, fists flailing and screeching, 'You beeeg ape! You leave my man alone!'

On another occasion, at the Mocambo, Errol Flynn punched out columnist Jimmy Fidler as payment for this item: 'Errol Flynn, whose love for his dog, Arno, has been much heralded, didn't even bother to get his body when it was washed ashore. That's how much he cared for him.' As Fidler went down, his wife leapt to her feet, grabbed a fork and plunged it into the flabbergasted star's ear.

Louis B. Mayer, a notorious one-punch artist, left a trail of crumpled bodies in his wake, though it's unlikely that many would have risked their future health and happiness by trading blows. Although Mayer was rumoured to have taken a rather more than fatherly interest in such stars as Myrna Loy, Jeanette MacDonald, Judy Garland and Lena Horne, he was a tireless public advocate of the sanctity of womanhood. During the shooting of *The Merry Widow* in 1928, director Erich von Stroheim casually referred to the character played by leading lady Mae Murray as a whore. LB exploded, 'I don't make pictures about whores!', to which the Beastly Hun, true to form, replied, 'All women are whores.' Mayer promptly laid him out.

The lobby of the Alexandria Hotel was the scene of a confrontation between Mayer and Charles Chaplin, whose chaotic sexual life and socialist politics were calculated to inflame the Brahma bull of the MGM boardroom. LB bore down on the diminutive Chaplin, blustering that the comedian had been spreading ugly rumours about his ex-wife Mildred Harris, who was then under contract to Mayer. Always a believer in getting his retaliation in first, Mayer silenced the protesting Chaplin with a single haymaker before lumbering on his way.

Lights . . . Camera . . . ACTION!

On many a set a boxing referee might have been more useful than a director. Rivalries between a studio's top stars were the very stuff of Hollywood gossip, spoonfed to the public by Hedda and Louella and not infrequently engineered by the studios themselves. In the early 1920s Paramount fomented a feud between their exotic foreign import Pola Negri and homegrown star Gloria Swanson. It was as phoney as Negri's name (she was born Barbara Appollonia Chalupiec), but it helped sell movies.

However, no one needed to stoke up the fires of an artificial quarrel when Bette Davis and Miriam Hopkins squared up to each other while making *Old Acquaintance* in 1943. Sparks also flew during the stormy filming of *The Women* in 1939. When Joan Crawford grabbed the role of the hardboiled vixen Crystal, she continued to play the part off the set, bitching her hated co-star Norma Shearer and being bawled out by director George Cukor.

Joan could drive anyone to distraction, but it never took much to excite the peppery Hungarian director Michael Curtiz. While directing *Mildred Pierce* (1945), he grew so frustrated with Crawford's tantrums that he tore the shoulder pads off her dress.

Curtiz was a hard-driving bully who was equally careless of the lives of the extras in the flood scene in *Noah's Ark* (1928) and the lives of the horses in *The Charge of the Light Brigade* (1936). He was famous for his mangled English, and colloquialisms every bit as extravagant as those uttered by Sam Goldwyn. While filming *The Charge of the Light Brigade*, Curtiz spotted David Niven at the side of the set, sharing a laugh with Errol Flynn about something he had just roared over his megaphone. Turning the loud-hailer towards the grinning actors, Curtiz bellowed, 'You think I know fucking nothing! Well let me tell you I know fuck all!'

'Difficult' stars are not unknown in these enlightened times, not the least of them the overbearing Barbra Streisand. As an ex-roommate once observed, 'Barbra has settled for more.' Inevitably this means that others get less of everything, particularly co-operation. After she had stomped furiously off the set of *Hello Dolly!* for the umpteenth time, exasperated co-star Walter Matthau yelled after her, 'Just remember, Betty Hutton once thought *she* was indispensable!' and was greeted with a round of applause from the assembled technicians. After another violent altercation he delivered himself of the understandable if hyperbolic opinion: 'I have more talent in one of my farts than you do in the whole of your body!' After the filming was over, he reflected, 'I have no disagreement with Barbra Streisand. I was merely exasperated by her tendency towards megalomania.'

Fun and Games with Roman

Directors frequently suffer at the hands of temperamental stars and producers. After the troubled filming of *Macbeth* in 1971, director Roman Polanski sent producer Victor Lownes a solid gold prick as a mark of his esteem.

Revenge can sometimes be exacted on the set. On *Cul-de-Sac* (1968) relations between Polanski and gravel-voiced character actor Lionel Stander were somewhat strained. One day over lunch Polanski asked Stander if he could drink a bottle of milk in one go. 'Sure!' replied Stander, grabbing the nearest bottle and gulping it down without a pause. When he had finished, Polanski looked up from consulting his watch and said, 'Fantastic! Eleven seconds. Can you do that when we shoot?' 'Sure!' replied Stander. It took 16 takes – 16 pints of milk – before Polanski was satisfied. In another scene Polanski forced Stander to eat 22 raw eggs.

Filming with Polanski is never less than lively. On *Chinatown* (1974) the excitable little director found Jack Nicholson watching baseball on a portable television when he was urgently needed on set. Seizing an iron bar he began to smash up the television while Nicholson, incandescent with rage, tore off all his clothes in front of the crew. Shooting had to be abandoned as by now both men were too hysterical to resume work. On the same film, Polanski was constantly at odds with Faye Dunaway over the interpretation of the femme fatale she was playing. To annoy her between takes, he recited Rimbaud to her in French.

Sometimes the boot is on the other foot. James Cagney once flattened a director who persisted in making him repeat a simple line. He then phoned Jack Warner and told him, 'You can come and pick up your boy – I just laid him out.'

Lee Marvin, berated by Joshua Logan for his drunken antics on *Paint Your Wagon* (1969), responded by urinating all over the director's boots.

The Face on the Cutting Room Floor

The ultimate sanction is consignment to the cutting room floor. When Buster Keaton threatened to upstage Charles Chaplin in the scene they shared in Chaplin's *Limelight* (1952), the Great Stoneface's best moments were slashed from the film.

John Ireland never became a top-line star, although he had his chances, notably in Howard Hawks's *Red River* (1948), which might have given him a big break had not his role been drastically cut during production. The film's screenwriter Chase Borden claimed that Hawks reached for the guillotine to punish Ireland for rustling the film's leading lady, Joanne Dru, from his own corral. As Hawks was married at the time, revenge had to be clandestine.

The beans were spilled when Chase lunched with Hawks and the film's star John Wayne. While Hawks was in the men's room, Wayne told the writer that Ireland's character was going to be dropped from the film because 'he's fooling around with Howard's girl'. Chase protested, 'What the hell's that got to do with making a picture! I don't care if he's fooling around with the Virgin Mary, you've got a picture to make and the guy's good!' Wayne replied, 'He's out and that's it.'

Hawks stonewalled when challenged about the vendetta, claiming that he was sick of Ireland's late-night drinking and pot-smoking sessions, which left him more than a little fuzzy when it came to an early-morning call. Nevertheless, Ireland disappears over the horizon for long sections of *Red River*. When he finally reappears, it is for the sole purpose of being casually gunned down by John Wayne. Hawks's pettiness availed him nothing, as Dru and Ireland were married shortly after completing the film.

Upstage, Downstage

The heavyweight German star Emil Jannings resorted to more brutal methods with Marlene Dietrich when filming Josef von Sternberg's *The Blue Angel* (1930), the movie which made Marlene a star.

In the late 1920s Jannings had hovered portentously over Hollywood like a giant Zeppelin, the legend 'Great Actor' emblazoned in Gothic script on its sides. But the talkies had revealed Jannings's thick German accent and he was packed back to the Fatherland by Paramount clutching the Academy Award he had won in 1928 for his performance as the broken Tsarist general in *The Last Command*.

In *The Blue Angel*, Jannings played the stuffy schoolmaster bewitched then broken and humiliated by Marlene's incomparable nightclub slut Lola-Lola. Halfway through shooting Jannings realized that the film was being effortlessly stolen from him by a woman who didn't seem to be acting at all. Therein, of course, lies the mystery of cinema. Hysterical with rage, the 'Great Actor' burst into von Sternberg's office, moaning, holding his head and railing against that 'nincompoop idiot fool I'm working with!' Somewhat less than tactfully it was pointed out that it was he, the great Emil Jannings, who had requested Dietrich in the first place. He decided quite literally to take matters into his own hands.

In the scene in which he was to attack Lola-Lola, he seized Dietrich and flung her on a couch, his stubby fingers in a vice-like grip around her neck. Marlene fought to break free, but Jannings was not about to let go. Suddenly von Sternberg realized that this was for real. Jannings had flipped and was really trying to throttle his co-star. He rushed onto the set and dragged off the hulking actor, who was promptly struck in the face by Hans Albers. Jannings dissolved into tears and stumbled from the set. Marlene, whose genuine terror is plain to see in the finished film, was rushed to her dressing room and revived. She bore the bruises on her neck for several weeks, and Jannings narrowly escaped an attempted murder rap.

Joan Crawford took stern measures against Mercedes McCambridge while making Nicholas Ray's baroque Western *Johnny Guitar* (1954). Mercedes's bravura acting style was clearly stealing Joan's thunder as well as winning spontaneous applause from the crew. Joan went on the war-path, and to avoid battle royal on the set Nicholas Ray was obliged to shoot McCambridge's scenes at the crack of dawn. Spying on an early-morning shoot, Joan's paranoia was confirmed. The bitch was upstaging her! Medusa eyes ablaze, she stalked off to her rival's dressing room and proceeded to shred all her costumes to ribbons. Not content with this, Joan spent the next two years trying to make sure that Mercedes never worked in Hollywood again.

Two of the greatest upstagers of all time, Mae West and W. C. Fields, were paired for the first and last time in *My Little Chickadee* (1940), the comedy equivalent of *King Kong v. Godzilla*. Throughout production the stars sniped away at each other. Of the bibulous Fields, Mae observed: 'There is no one quite like Bill. And it would be snide of me to add, "Thank God". A great performer. My only doubts about him come in bottles.' Precisely, Mae. Fields won the bout on a technical knockout, slyly filching Mae's most famous line and asking her to 'come up and see me some time. . . in Philadelphia!'

Fields's magnificently bleary eye focused with unfailing accuracy on the absurdities and pettiness of life. Drink-sodden, florid of speech and nose, a relentless misogynist and child hater, he reserved a special place in his demonology for women and children. He had a special way of dealing with his tiny antagonist Baby LeRoy, the child star with whom he first locked horns in *Tillie and Gus* (1933). When asked about his small co-star, the curmudgeonly Fields replied, 'Fella named LeRoy, *claims* he's a baby.' On one famous occasion he spiked LeRoy's orange juice with gin. When the liquor began to take effect and Baby was carried away, Fields strutted round the set, triumphantly proclaiming, 'The kid's no trouper!'

Marlene Dietrich was the focus of an equally infantile feud between her co-stars Edward G. Robinson and George Raft when they were making *Manpower* (1941). Both men had the hots for Dietrich, although the enigmatic Marlene was not going to lay. She preferred lanky all-American types like John Wayne and Jimmy Stewart. The needle between Raft and Robinson was increased by the latter's niggling advice to Raft on the best way to deliver his lines and handle business. The tension finally exploded into a punch-up on the set which was captured by a *Life* photographer.

Raft was ever-ready with a swift right. Two years later, on *Background to Danger*, he filmed a scene in which he was tied to a chair by heavies Peter Lorre and Sydney Greenstreet. Lorre enjoyed himself hugely, laughing sadistically and blowing cigarette smoke into Raft's eyes. As soon as he was untied, Raft made straight for Lorre's dressing room and decked the diminutive character star.

Edward G. Robinson picked on someone his own size when he was filming *Barbary Coast* (1935) with Miriam Hopkins. He considered Hopkins 'Puerile, silly and snobbish', an opinion confirmed by her insistence on wearing a series of elaborate costumes which made Robinson look even more dwarf-like than usual. To add insult to injury, she demanded a box for him to stand on during their scenes together. When the script called for Edward G. to slap Hopkins on the cheek, he floored her with a right uppercut to the jaw.

Ever the 'serious actress', Bette Davis wanted Laurence Olivier as her co-star in *The Private Lives of Elizabeth and Essex* (1939). Instead she got Errol Flynn. Not in the same league, my dear, and, to boot, on a higher salary than the smouldering Davis. Bette relieved her disappointment on the set by delivering a 'stage slap' to Flynn of such force that the brittle he-man was knocked cold.

Try as they might, some stars just never hit it off. Laurence Olivier was determined that Vivien Leigh should appear opposite him in *Rebecca* (1940). Producer David O. Selznick wouldn't play ball. After Scarlett O'Hara, the mousey little heroine of *Rebecca* was just too big a character change. Moreover, Selznick felt that the public might react unfavourably to real-life lovers Olivier and Leigh smooching on screen, particularly as they were both married to other people at the time. So Larry got Joan Fontaine, who had to endure the stream of obscenities he whispered into her ear during their screen clinches. Sadistic director Alfred Hitchcock played along with it all, as Fontaine's obvious distress conveyed precisely the vulnerability for which he was searching.

The sweet nothings Spencer Tracy whispered into the ear of starchy Irene Dunne while they were filming *A Guy Named Joe* (1943) were of an equally explicit nature. Grumpy, hard-drinking Spence was strongly attracted to *noli me tangere* types like Dunne and, most famously, Katharine Hepburn. When the script called for canoodling, Tracy gave Dunne a graphically detailed description of what he really wanted to do with her. Studio boss Louis B. Mayer had to be called in to read the riot act to his horny leading man.

Vivien Leigh had a different close-up problem with Clark Gable while making *Gone With the Wind* (1939). Her love scenes with the 'King' were made almost unendurable by the blasts of fetid breath caused by his less than satisfactory dentures. Twenty-five years later, while making *Ship of Fools*, Leigh had an equally distressing close encounter of the vaporous kind with Lee Marvin when she was stiffed by his alcohol-scented attentions.

Diplomatic Fred Astaire always refused to be drawn on which of his leading ladies was his favourite dancing partner, although it was well known that there was little love lost between him and Ginger Rogers. In the 1970s he politely declined an invitation to a reunion with Ginger at a Lincoln Center tribute, leaving his erstwhile co-star to kiss a top hat for the benefit of the press. As Fred once admitted to the actress Dana Wynter, 'Ginger was *so* heavy!'

RED SCARES IN THE SUNSET

In the beginning there was the Second World War. And in the Second World War the United States and the Soviet Union were allies. As part of its war effort, Hollywood made a string of movies hymning the courageous Russians' fight against Fascism. Some, like Michael Curtiz's *Mission to Moscow* (1943) were examples of brilliantly manipulative propaganda. Others were pure hokum: who can

Robert Taylor swearing in before the House of Un-American Activities.

forget the sight of comely Russian partisans Gregory Peck and Tamara Toumanova prettily lobbing grenades at Nazi tanks in *Days of Glory* (1944)?; or the intriguing spectacle of Robert Taylor conducting a Soviet symphony orchestra in *Song of Russia* (1943)?

However, when the guns fell silent in Berlin, a new shadow fell over Europe. Adolf Hitler's ashes had barely had time to cool before the 'Cold War' began. The Soviet ally was now an enemy. Genial 'Uncle Joe' Stalin was once again a monster, his hands dripping blood.

Nor was there much comfort to be gained from the way in which the war in the Far East had been brought to an end. With the destruction by atomic bombs of the Japanese cities of Hiroshima and Nagasaki, the Second World War had been terminated in a manner universally acknowledged as the harbinger of even more terrible conflicts to come. For the moment the United States held a monopoly of nuclear weapons, but how long would that monopoly last?

In the United States, postwar unease, fear of the Soviet Union, and fear of subversion from within, encouraged an undercurrent of paranoia. In the new political climate, Hollywood's wartime celebrations of the Soviet way of life became deeply embarrassing to the studio bosses. The sweat stood out on Jack Warner's forehead every time he thought of *Mission to Moscow*. Robert Taylor announced that he had made *Song of Russia* under protest.

Are You Now or Have You Ever Been. . .?

It did not take long for the tentacles of rabid Red-baiting politics to spread through Hollywood. In 1945 there had been a series of labour disputes at the major studios, which in October climaxed in a riot outside the Warner studios at Burbank. A year later trouble flared again, with skirmishing between police and pickets breaking out at Warners and MGM.

In 1947 the House Un-American Activities Committee (HUAC) moved in on Hollywood, convinced that the labour unrest had been Communist-inspired. HUAC had been formed in 1937 and in 1940 was conducting investigations into Hollywood under the chairmanship of Texas Democrat Martin Dies, a man so right-wing that he practically disappeared off the political Richter scale. At one point he even suspected Shirley Temple of being a Communist! Defiant anti-intellectualism was the order of the day on HUAC. At one hearing a witness unwisely quoted the Elizabethan poet Christopher Marlowe, whereupon he was interrupted by Joe Starnes, Dies's henchman, who rasped, 'You are quoting from this Marlowe. Is he a Communist?' In the postwar years HUAC's principal role was the exploitation of public ignorance and hysteria about 'Communist conspiracy'. Officially, its members had the power only to suggest alterations to any new law. In fact, HUAC had the power to wreck people's lives, using innuendo, hearsay and malice, under the protective umbrella of the right-wing press.

Prominent among HUAC's supporters in the press was columnist Hedda Hopper, who was stomping the country addressing women's clubs, urging them to boycott films which featured 'Communist actors'. Hedda was also made Vice-President of the Motion Picture Alliance for the Preservation of American Ideals, among whose leading lights were director Leo McCarey and actors John Wayne, Ward Bond, Robert Taylor and Hollywood's self-appointed 'expert' on Communism, Adolphe Menjou. Adolphe was firmly of the opinion that sneaky Red actors could infiltrate Communist notions into a film merely by the inflection they cunningly gave their lines. He predicted that a Communist take-over of the United States was imminent and declared that he was going to live in Texas 'because the Texans will shoot all Communists on sight'. Clearly it did not occur to him that the good ol' boys of the Lone Star State might just as easily gun down dandified little Hollywood actors when they appeared on the horizon.

Menjou's penetrating insights into the Red menace set the intellectual tone of the HUAC hearings, which opened privately in the spring of 1947. Its chairman was J. Parnell Thomas, a corrupt reactionary who was later jailed for payroll padding. One of the more pernicious members of the Committee was the anti-Semitic Mississippi Congressman John Rankin, who announced his dismay on discovering that Danny Kaye's real name was Daniel Kaminsky. It would have been laughable if the consequences of HUAC's deliberations had not been so tragic.

HUAC discovered that there was no shortage of 'friendly' witnesses. Ginger Rogers's monstrous mother Lela proudly told the Committee of her daughter's patriotic refusal to deliver the line 'Share and share alike – that's democracy', in *Tender Comrade* (1943), a piece of wartime moral uplift about women war workers. Sharing things? Good heavens, we can't have any of that in the land of the free!

Gary Cooper stepped forward to provide a critique of Communism straight from *Mr Deeds Goes to Town*: 'From what I hear of it, I don't like it, because it isn't on the level', a sentiment which might well have been applied to HUAC itself. Was Gary worried that someone might remember that in the more innocent days of 1938 he was voted top male star in a poll of the delegates to the American Communist Party's national convention taken by the *Daily Worker*? (That well-known fellow-traveller Claudette Colbert was their favourite leading lady.)

Robert Montgomery told the Committee, 'I gave up my job to fight a totalitarianism called Fascism. I am ready to do it again to fight the totalitarianism called Communism.'

After the 23 'friendly' witnesses came the turn of 19 'unfriendly' witnesses. Of these, eight writers, a producer and a director – who became known as the 'Hollywood Ten' – declined to testify before the Committee and were held in contempt of Congress.

The Hollywood Ten were John Howard Lawson, Dalton Trumbo, Lester Cole, Alvah Bessie, Albert Maltz, Ring Lardner Jr, Samuel Ornitz, Herbert J. Biberman, Edward Dmytryk and Adrian Scott. They were by no means insubstantial figures. Scott and Dmytryk were RKO's top producer-director team, riding high on the success of *Crossfire*, a hard-hitting indictment of anti-Semitism and the studio's most profitable film of 1947. Dalton Trumbo was one of the highest-paid screenwriters in Hollywood, and among his credits were *A Guy Named Joe* (1943), *Thirty Seconds over Tokyo* (1944) and Ginger Rogers's favourite film, *Tender Comrade*. Ring Lardner's credits included *Woman of the Year* (1942), *The Cross of Lorraine* (1943) and *Tomorrow the World* (1944).

Under the leadership of John Howard Lawson the Ten refused to answer the question: 'Are you now, or have you ever been a Communist?' Rather than refuse to testify on the grounds that they might incriminate themselves (according to the Fifth

Amendment), they regarded the Committee itself as unconstitutional. Lawson stated, 'I am not on trial here . . . the Committee is on trial before the American people.'

A Committee for the First Amendment, chaired by John Huston, was formed to protest against HUAC's infringement of the constitutional rights of the Hollywood Ten. A planeload of stars, among them Humphrey Bogart, Lauren Bacall, Richard Conte and Danny Kaye, flew to Washington in a blaze of publicity. However, they quickly caved in when pressure was applied by the Truman administration.

According to the writer-director Abraham Polonsky, soon to become another victim of the Red purge: 'General Beadle Smith was sent to Hollywood and he met the important Hollywood owners. A policy was laid down to call these stars and directors off – the important ones. Pressure was put on them through their agents and the whole thing melted in about two weeks. I finally went down to a meeting and Humphrey Bogart turned around and looked up a half empty room; the first meetings were held at George Chasen's, and you couldn't get in – it was like an opening night at the opera – everybody wanted to be in on this. Anyway, Humphrey Bogart looked round this room and said: "You don't think I'm going to stand up there all by myself and take a beating – I'm getting out too." And he walked out of the room. Then Huston said, "Well, it's hopeless, fellows," and left for Europe. The final meeting was held and the only people present were Willie Wyler, the permanent secretary, myself and one other. Wyler said, "Well, I think we can use our time better than this." And it was true.'

The industry did not lift a finger to help the Hollywood Ten. In November 1947, at a meeting in New York, the Association of Motion Picture Producers declared that the Ten had 'impaired their usefulness to the industry', a phrase of which Stalin himself might have been proud, and that they would not be re-employed until they had purged themselves of the contempt and sworn under oath that they were not Communists. The Association went on to pledge that the industry would not 'knowingly employ a Communist or a member of any party or group which advocates the overthrow of the Government of the United States by force or by any illegal or unconstitutional method'. Thus began the dreaded 'blacklist', on which were placed the names of writers, directors and actors who were suspected of the slightest traces of left-wing sympathies.

A surprising opponent of HUAC was Sam Goldwyn, no lover of Communism but a man who felt that the gathering witch-hunt was itself un-American. Goldwyn thought that those in Hollywood making the most noise about the Communist threat – men like Louis B. Mayer and Jack Warner – were blustering hypocrites. They had been happy to sanction films like *Song of Russia* and *Mission to Moscow* during the War and could not disown them. Goldwyn intervened to prevent a close friend, the screenwriter Robert Sherwood, from being hauled before the Committee to explain certain 'suspect scenes' in, of all films, the Oscar-laden hit *The Best Years of Our Lives* (1946).

Sherwood was luckier than the Hollywood Ten, who underwent a prolonged legal agony. The proceedings against them dragged on for over two years before any of them served time in prison. Then, in 1949, Red mania exploded on the front pages in even more virulent form, with the conviction of the former State Department official Alger Hiss on a charge of espionage – the first major political triumph of a young Republican Congressman, Richard Milhouse Nixon.

Politicians in both the Republican and Democrat Parties were now convinced that the very fabric of government was infested with Communist infiltrators. Perhaps the entire State Department was a nest of spies: could Franklin Delano Roosevelt have been a crypto-Commie?; and what about Harry Truman? In these feverish times anything seemed possible to those blinkered by bigotry. Fuel was added to the flames when the Korean War broke out in June 1950.

HUAC remained the focus of the witch-hunt, but numerous self-appointed committees now sprang up like mushrooms, combing libraries and bookstores for Red propaganda. Reactionary sheets like *Red Channels* and the pamphlets issued by the Catholic Information Society fingered celebrities who had supported liberal causes and Communist 'front' organizations. Their model was *The Red Network*, published in the early 1930s by a fanatical right-winger, Elizabeth Dilling, who believed that the YMCA was a Communist 'front' and that Eleanor Roosevelt was a 'dangerous pacifist'.

And then there was Joseph McCarthy, an obscure junior Senator from Wisconsin, who on 9 February 1950 delivered a speech to the Women's Republican Club in Wheeling, West Virginia, in which he claimed to be in possession of a list of 205 employees of the State Department who were known to the Secretary of State Dean Acheson to be card-carrying Communists. In Wheeling itself, where McCarthy's campaign began, public-spirited citizens made a shattering discovery. Inside packets of a certain brand of ideologically sound US bubble gum were give-away cards informing unwary schoolchildren that the USSR, with its population of 211 million, had its capital in Moscow and was 'the largest country in the world'. The very foundations of democracy were trembling. The bubble-gum cards were seized and burnt.

After the bonfire a Mrs Thomas J. White, who sat on the Indiana State Textbook Commission, declared: 'There is a Communist directive now to stress the story of Robin Hood. . . because he robbed the rich and gave it to the poor. That's the Communist line. It's just a smearing of law and order.'

McCarthy's bullying 'inquiries' lasted until April 1954, when the American people finally grew weary of him. It would be cheering to think that an overwhelming revulsion swept him away, but the truth is that McCarthy was one of the first great casualties of over-exposure on television. People simply grew bored with him.

Scoundrel Time

In the years between 1947 and 1954 fear and betrayal spread their poison throughout Hollywood. Notable victims of the blacklist included actors John Garfield, Anne Revere, Gale Sondergaard, Marsha Hunt, Howard Da Silva and Larry Parks. If you escaped the blacklist, you might still run foul of the 'greylist' compiled by the American Legion. To buy yourself off the list, it was necessary to make grovelling confessions of guilt and to 'name names', feeding the ever-growing cancer.

One of the Hollywood Ten, Edward Dmytryk, finally cracked and 'named' the director John Berry, who in 1950 had made a documentary supporting the Ten. Along with fellow-director Joseph Losey and writer Carl Foreman, Berry refused to testify and left for Europe. Losey had a nasty turn in England not long afterwards when he suddenly spied Ginger Rogers's mother Lela stalking through the studio where he was working under the borrowed name of 'Victor Hanbury'. Fortunately for cinema, the old gorgon failed to spot him and a distinguished career was saved from further blight.

In contrast, the resilient Dalton Trumbo stayed in America and kept working. He wrote in *The Nation* in 1957: 'The studios, while operating a blacklist, were in the market purchasing plays and other material without crediting the authors.' After all, business is business. In 1957, as 'Robert Rich', Trumbo wrote the Oscar-winning screenplay for *The Brave One*. The Award went unclaimed until 1975.

A blacklisted writer might use the name of a friend. This could lead to complications, a phenomenon brilliantly satirized in *The Front* (1976), in which Woody Allen played a schmuk enlisted by blacklisted writers to put his name to their scripts. The film's director, Martin Ritt, and three of its leading players, Zero Mostel, Herschel Bernardi and Lloyd Gough, had all been blacklisted in the 1950s.

There were plenty of hard-faced men who did well out of the Cold War, the investigators, consultants and self-styled experts on Communism who compiled the endless lists of suspects, usually on the flimsiest information.

Theirs was truly a self-perpetuating profession; there could be no end to the lists, or there would be no job.

Studios employed detective agencies to compile dossiers on their employees. At RKO Howard Hughes devised a 'loyalty test' for suspect directors, offering them a truly ghastly property, *I Married a Communist*, as a test of their political reliability. The game of pass the parcel continued until the dreary package came to rest in the hands of Robert Stevenson, who had no qualms about such things. Released in 1950 as *The Woman on Pier 13*, it made a thumping $650,000 loss for the studio.

Hollywood hit the high-water mark of its anti-Communist crusade in 1952, when thirteen Red-bashing films were released. By far the wildest and the woolliest was *Red Planet Mars*, in which clean-cut Peter Graves discovers that God is broadcasting to us from Mars. Earth is gripped by a religious revival, and the Communist regime in Russia is swept aside by a theocracy run by a clutch of bearded Khomeini lookalikes. The advent of the millennium is then threatened by the appearance of a crazed drink-sodden scientist – a former Nazi now in the pay of the Soviets – who claims that not only is Graves's receiving equipment based on his own wartime experiments but also that he is responsible for all the uplifting interplanetary messages. Graves solves this tricky problem by blowing himself, the Communist and his young wife to smithereens in his laboratory – but not before the final message comes over the line, 'Well done, thou good and faithful servant'!

'Is This the End of Edward G?'

The hysterical convolutions of *Red Planet Mars* are good for a laugh, but the fate of those on the blacklist was less risible. One of its most famous victims was Edward G. Robinson, who in his memoirs *All My Yesterdays* recalled in anguished detail the misery he endured in the late 1940s and early 1950s as he fought to save his career from the smears of the Red-baiters.

Robinson had always been a political liberal, and in the 1930s and wartime years had lent his name and his money to a number of progressive causes. This idealistic generosity was to cost him dear in the witch-hunt that followed.

Robinson discovered that the (California) Senate Fact-Finding Committee on Un-American Activities had released a report, 'Repudiations and Denials of Communism', which contained a list of individuals investigated during its deliberations. Robinson's name was on the list, categorized as a supporter of a number of Communist 'front' organizations. Attacks quickly followed in *Red Channels* and Hedda Hopper's column in *The Hollywood Reporter*.

Work began to dry up, a process which Robinson later divided into six distinct stages:

'My agent, in the way of agents, went the way of all agents in dealing with a once hot and now cooling actor:

> *Phase 1:* "Hell, Eddie, I've read a lot of scripts submitted for you, and there isn't one that's right for you. Nothing but the best for you, Eddie, baby. You know that."
> *Phase 2:* "Business in lots of trouble, Eddie, baby. Postwar adjustment and all that crap. I've got something really hot cooking. Believe me, baby."
> *Phase 3:* "Eddie, it's not so easy at your age. Character parts, you know. After all, you're not exactly a baby, are you, Eddie?"
> *Phase 4:* "There seems to be some opposition to you, Eddie. I'm looking into it. Whatever it is, we'll fight it with every penny we've got. You know that."
> *Phase 5* (coming from the agent's secretary): "I'm sorry, Mr Robinson, but Mr B is out of town. I'll give him your message. He'll certainly call you at his earliest convenience."
> *Phase 6:* No earliest convenience.

Robinson was added to the American Legion's 'greylist'. His post was filled with obscene anti-Semitic hate mail, of which this is an example: 'Yiddish Riff-Raff – From stinking European ghettoes – Call Him or His Followers names – Far worse than you are being called today? Didn't you and your wife visit Trotsky in Mexico – Shortly before his assassination? Were you – the "Finger Man" in that "Rub-Out" H-M-M? – Jew? it's too late – Jew! – Nothing that you and "Cantor" – Issy Ishkovitz! – can say or do – will be accepted by the Christian-American public! You and the Skunk-Jew-Riff-Raff of Hollywood – have overplayed your hand! – We . . . know you now! – We're not gonna rest – until you scum – are driven out of the "Entertainment Field" – Every dog – has his day – You Kikes . . . had yours too long! Now it's our turn!. . .

Robinson flapped around helplessly, unable to clear his name. Work came and then went with the publication of new smears and the circulation of fresh rumours. Survival had become a wholly arbitrary affair.

In response to an appeal by the imprisoned Dalton Trumbo, Robinson sent a cheque for $2,500 to his wife. Somehow this act of charity came to the attention of Robinson's persecutors. He received a visit from Victor Lasky, a newspaperman, publicist and fanatical anti-Communist. Lasky taxed Robinson with his folly in sending the cheque to the Trumbo family and with his support for Communist 'front' organizations: 'He was particularly miserable about my association with the American Committee for the Protection of Foreign Born, which he assured me was a Communist-dominated front, thus implying that its active members, including Reinhold Niebuhr, Dorothy

Thompson and William Allen White, were either Communists or dupes.

'Dupes. Yes, that was the word. All I had to do to clear myself of all these charges, new and old, was to admit publicly and in print that I was a dupe. And he, Victor Lasky, would write it all out for me and secure its publication in some nice conservative journal like, I supposed, *American Legion* magazine.

'He prepared 26 pages of my dupedom. I only had to read one page to feel the urge to throw up.

'I told Mr Lasky politely and firmly that I wished no part of his attempt to set the world straight, though firms of lawyers I had engaged in New York and Los Angeles were not at all sure that it wasn't a good idea. The piece he fashioned made me out a fool who out of brainlessness and overzealous consideration for mankind had been blindly led into organizations that wished to destroy America.'

At this stage Robinson still had the guts to send Lasky packing. But many of those under threat chose this humiliating method of working their way back to respectability. Broken and with his career in ruins, John Garfield put his name to an article which confessed: 'I Was a Sucker for a Left Hook.'

Finally, a similar humiliation was visited on Robinson who could stand no more. In April 1952, testifying for the third time before HUAC, Robinson confessed his dupedom and named names, prompting this observation from the Committee's chairman Francis Walter: 'Well, actually this Committee has never had any evidence presented to indicate that you were anything more than a very choice sucker. I think you are number one on the sucker list of this country.'

The 'number one sucker' clawed his way back with theatre work (the lead in the ironically appropriate adaptation of Arthur Koestler's *Darkness at Noon*) and a string of B-movies. Some of these modest little programmers, notably *Illegal* (1955), now look better than many of the A-features of the period. Robinson's return to the fold was signalled by a big featured role in Cecil B. DeMille's *The Ten Commandments* (1956). The scars, however, never healed.

Garfield's public recantation had been too late. He died from a heart attack in 1952, not long after the publication of the article with which he hoped to buy back his career. He had been in New York, rehearsing for a revival of Clifford Odets' Golden Boy, the play in which he had first come to the attention of Hollywood in 1937. Of his sad final years a friend observed: 'The tragedy was that Garfield wasn't accused of anything. He was a street boy with a street boy's sense of honour, and when they asked him to give the names of friends at parties he refused. They blacklisted him for that. When he wasn't able to work he ran around in a violent, stupid kind of way. In the end he died of a heart attack. The blacklist killed him.'

DON'T LOOK NOW

British film censors have never been afraid of using the term censorship. In America, however, a country which tends to wear democracy on its sleeve, censorship has always proved an unpalatable concept, even though it has always been a fighting force in American film culture. The idea of a National Board of Film Censors would be unacceptable to most Americans.

On the other hand, there are an increasing number of noisy pressure groups who view censorship as a positive ally and would like to have control over even the slightest screen gesture which affronted their sensibilities. Naturally Hollywood can't afford to ignore these good people since they might severely dent its profits.

Art for Art's Sake, Money for Christ's Sake

Yet sometimes they can unintentionally boost them. The most recent Hollywood furore stemmed from Martin Scorsese's *The Last Temptation of Christ*. Even while shooting was still in full swing, stories leaked out about the film's alleged debunking of Christ and glimpses of his sex life. The film, which twins Willem Defoe as Jesus and Barbara Hershey as Mary Magdalene, also portrayed a 'wimpish' Christ in the eyes of the fundamentalists. Their consequent actions served to underline both their single-minded vigour as well as their financial clout.

First they offered to reimburse Universal for their $10 million plus expenditure on the film, so they could collect all the copies which they would then ceremoniously burn. Universal hit back via a series of newspaper advertisements:

> While we understand the deep feelings which have prompted this offer, we believe that to accept it would threaten the fundamental freedoms of religion and expression promised to all Americans under our Constitution.
>
> In the United States no one sect or coalition has the power to set boundaries around each person's freedom to explore religious or philosophical questions whether through speech, books, or film.
>
> These freedoms protect us all. They are precious. They are not for sale.

The reply from the aggrieved was as solid as ever. They felt the plans by MCA chairman Lew Wasserman and president Sid Sheinberg to proceed with the film's release would 'fan the flames of anti-Semitism'. In other words the real sub-text was simply that two Jews (Wasserman and Sheinberg) had no business touching a picture which questioned the nature of Jesus Christ.

Aside from protests outside the Burbank offices of MCA, there were also anti-Jewish demonstrations outside the home of Wasserman himself. The Christians flew an airplane over his roof with a banner which proclaimed, 'Wasserman fans Jew hatred with Temptation'. Next they delivered an effigy of a blood-spattered Christ being ground into the earth by a businessman.

Jack Valenti, President of the Motion Picture Association of America, lent his muscle to the fight by helping Universal: 'No one,' he said, 'no matter how passionate their opposition, can or should prevent the entry of a point of view, whether it is creative, political or philosophical.'

On his side were a group of mainstream churchmen, none of whom, having been shown an unfinished version of the film by Scorsese, believed that it ought to be banned.

Scorsese, himself a deeply spiritual man who once trained for the priesthood, is the last director to make a two-cents version of the Christ story. You only have to examine his previous output to witness his obsession with the conflict between body and soul, material and spiritual. This did not deter the protesters who deemed it unnecessary to view a single frame of film.

Scorsese was clearly disturbed by the strength of the protests. He

sincerely claimed that the film had been made 'with deep religious feeling. I believe it is a film about suffering and the struggle to find God. It was made with conviction and love, and so I believe it is an affirmation of faith, not a denial.'

'Further,' he went on, 'I feel strongly that people everywhere will be able to identify with the human side of Jesus as well as his divine side. I urge everyone to withhold judgement until we are able to screen the completed film.'

Marlon Brando and Maria Schneider in scene from controversial *Last Tango in Paris*.

The Last Temptation of Christ was eventually released in the States in late September 1988 and in Britain shortly afterwards. Thankfully a planet away from the biblical epics in which actors talked to the sky, it is a personal look at the self-doubts which may well have gripped Jesus-the-man when asked to be Jesus-the-son-of-God. The censorious Christian zealots were eventually trampled underfoot and the producers cleaned up. Useful publicity full marks; outraged protesters zero.

Otto's Blue Heaven

The official censors are as capable of being reduced to cloth-headed fools forced to stare at their shoes in embarrassment as they are of stalking the film industry as power-barons.

The Moon is Blue is a film which can still cause ageing censors to squirm and current censors to laugh with relief that it wasn't a hot potato which they were forced to handle.

A 1953 picture by Otto Preminger, based on the popular stage play by F. Hugh Herbert, it was refused a certificate by the Production Code Administration and roundly condemned by the Legion of Decency. After subsequent appeal it was turned down by the Board of Directors of the Motion Picture Association. United Artists, in order to release the film, were compelled to resign from the Association. Despite the pompous outrage and loud protests, they soon achieved a smash hit.

Most folk believe that blue language was the reason for the censor's frown. The carefree manner in which sex was discussed just had to be the reason. 'Virgin', 'pregnant' and 'seduce' were used, the staid *New York Times* declared, 'with bland insouciance and cool forthrightness.'

This was, in fact, not the problem. The crew and cast themselves experienced the thrill of being daring in this heady enterprise. In an interview at the time, the film's star, William Holden, said that he and Preminger had agreed beforehand that the script would not be sent over to the PCA Office for approval. Holden claimed that 'he didn't see anything unmoral (sic) about the picture'. Yet the fact that they had made an agreement beforehand made this supposed surprise at the later reaction to the film seem just a mite insincere. Anyhow some unknown, intentionally or otherwise, ensured that the script slipped into the judgemental hands of the PCA in late 1952. Their New Year's present to Preminger was a reply in early 1953.

There were, for sure, objections to certain words or phrases; for example, 'the broken expression "son of a . . . " is unacceptable'. Yet deeper objections arose not from total recoil from the language but from the moral degeneracy implicit in the story.

'The reference to marijuana should be omitted' was an instruction which set the fiery agenda. The upright censors were affronted by any number of lines whose language was perfectly acceptable but whose tone was deemed morally offensive: 'Men are usually bored with virgins', 'Godliness does not appeal to me', topped up by, 'steaks, liquor and sex – in that order', did not endear Holden and Preminger to the PCA finger-waggers.

Specifically, the hoo-ha arose from the plot. To describe it in synopsis is to make it sound like lunatic farce, but its hard-edged passion should never be in doubt.

William Holden plays an architect who has just had a frolic with Dawn Addams, the girl upstairs and daughter of charming rogue David Niven. Addams returns home to find her dad in the horizontal with his latest pick-up, so she runs downstairs and batters on Holden's door for a place to sleep. Holden, gent to the last, offers up his bed and disappears to the living room to claim the sofa.

After a bout of misunderstanding Holden admits that lofty principles and high-minded chivalry had nothing to do with his decision to vacate the bedroom but simply that Dawn Addams had come on strong and so removed his masculine right to fix time, place and circumstance. To add weight to his argument he goes out and snaps up Maggie McNamara, a chattering would-be television actress.

The plot thus reveals the true hand of the frothing censors. Sexual love was no longer a subject for moral consideration, just a matter of day-to-day expediency. If Holden wished to pursue Addams into the bedroom, or sleep on the sofa instead, that was purely a matter of personal whim. A lady viewer of the film was one of the first complainants. She found that the film was so out of sync with America's sound moral base that she intended to ensure that the film was seen by the Un-American Activities Committee of the United States, whose jackboot tactics were effective in paralysing a generation of film-makers.

Outrage turned on a key clause in the Code's rulebook which demanded that 'pictures shall not infer that low forms of sex relationship are the accepted or common thing'. Though Preminger was not suggesting that the whole free world was indulging in thrusting antics of an immoral kind, he did seem to be implying that free love was acceptable. A debate consequently raged about the difference, if any, between 'accepted' and 'acceptable' during which Preminger and Holden were seen as casual conveyers of evil to the pure American public.

A further twist in the plot stretched the PCA to the limit. When he discovers that his daughter has spent the night in an alien bed, Niven storms downstairs to go the full fifteen rounds with Holden. At first thrown by the fact that nothing *has* happened, he then succumbs to a fit of pique because Holden *didn't* touch her and so knocked her vanity for six! So he decides to thrash Holden anyway.

Yet this was as nothing when compared to what was the crucial scene for the PCA. Waltzing through the sexy romps and evil encounters was the aggressively pure figure of Maggie McNamara. So strident does she become about her virginity that Holden snaps back at her for being a 'professional virgin'. When she asks him what this means, he retorts that she is always advertising her virginity. When she then wonders what on earth is wrong with that, he replies that those who advertise usually have something to sell. Putting her firmly in her place, this always secures a big laugh and is the best remembered sequence in the entire film. The trouble for the PCA and its supporters was just this: for them, McNamara is the only object of admiration in the film and yet she is depicted as an out-to-lunch oddball and dotty eccentric simply for keeping her legs crossed. Holden is the scamp who ought to be sent to church rather than a character who is so blatantly seen to win when he trounces Maggie.

PCA director Joe Breen believed the Code values were being severely threatened by this film. To give himself some credible back-up he wheeled in Hearst newspaper columnist, George Sokolsky, who was a no-nonsense defender of old-fashioned virtue. 'Sound as a nut' was the epithet given by Breen to Sokolsky who, within the PCA, was thereafter referred to as 'sound-as-a-nut Sokolsky'. The columnist duly wrote a column which tore the film to shreds.

The only individual close to the action whose morals were not offended was PCA man Geoff Shurlock. Though he was forced to write stinging letters to Preminger on the orders of Breen, his boss, he was quite different when in conversation with the film director. He vaguely suggested notions like 'integrity' and 'taste' to the point where Preminger believed he was now the owner of a docile poodle on a handy leash.

Preminger naturally fell in line with those who looked at the film sideways. Underwhelmed by the Holden character, they felt that the odds were stacked in Maggie's favour. Although admitting that she was a bit like an insurance salesman in flouting her rectitude, they yet believed her to be in the right and Holden in the wrong. They also pointed out that she does indeed land her man in the end without removing her undies once. In addition she neither smoked nor drank and worked honestly for a living. In this twisted reading of the film, virtue triumphed and Preminger was only too happy to concur.

It is important to stress, however, that Breen was no innocent who was out of touch with street-level thought. Even the secular press dropped its collective jaw at the brassy candour of the film.

The worldly trade magazine, *Showmen's Trade Review*, was adamant that to hear the words 'virgin' and 'seduce' for the first time on the big screen was, 'a shock even for the most sophisticated'. The *Motion Picture Daily* was quick to advise exhibitors: 'If your audiences are prepared to take . . . outspokenness, [they] will be amused. If your audiences are of a different stripe you'd better see this before your house falls in on you.'

The snotty London correspondent of *Variety* felt that the film would prove too boring to the English who 'don't take to unrelieved sex with the same enthusiasm as their counterparts in America.'

Catholics too were soon issuing stern warnings against a film they regarded as 'an occasion of sin'. They were reminded by their superiors not only to avoid it but to never again enter cinemas that had dared show it. John F. O'Hara, the Archbishop of Philadelphia, did in fact try to ban the film from his city.

Finally it was Judge Herman Moser who snapped at the censor's shins. Ordering them to license the film, he described it as 'a light comedy telling a tale of wide-eyed, brash, puppy-like innocence routing or converting to its side the forces of evil it encounters.'

It was a full eight years later, in 1961, that the picture received its certificate. Meanwhile it mocked the dour puritanism of the PCA by achieving distribution without a Code Seal and becoming a hefty hit in the process.

A Sale of Two Titties

Ten years before, in 1943, the censors found something solid to cling to in the shape of Jane Russell's chest which had a lead part in Howard Hughes' *The Outlaw*. Afraid that Jane's best friends might cause grown-ups to go home and have sex, they enjoyed themselves thoroughly in the midst of controversy and litigation. Director Hughes found it tough to keep his camera from peeking down Jane's dress, and, when the drooling public was generously allowed in to see the film six years later, they found a lukewarm western with Russell's red-hot cleavage.

Filth Dressed as Art?

Censors the world over had fun with *Last Tango in Paris*. A record opening in Paris was followed by the film's confiscation in Italy, after which a court in Bologna refused to believe that it took 'persistent delight in arousing base, libidinous instincts'. United Artists, meanwhile, sneaked it into small theatres in New York, Los Angeles, Boston, Washington, Philadelphia and Toronto.

The whole was confused by some critics who regarded the sweaty writhings of Marlon Brando and Maria Schneider as a movie milestone and others who regarded it as filth dressed as art. Bernardo Bertolucci, the director, pretentious as ever, played to the gallery of jabbering TV celebrities who had now joined in the spectacle, by exclaiming: 'Pornography is not in the hands of the child who discovers his sexuality by masturbating, but in the hands of the adult who slaps him.' Quite.

For once one almost felt sorry for the censors as they slithered in the mud, desperately trying to shape public taste. Emerging in this case as perplexed humans, they are more often regarded as well-dressed bores who live in a cupboard.

OSCAR BITES ITS BEST

The annual Academy Awards are excellent at revealing to the world just what a lonely place Hollywood can be. Due to highly selective directing and severe editing we witness every year a succession of gleaming teeth which proceed to chatter non-stop, thanking the third tea boy twice removed without whom such-and-such a picture (any title will do) could not possibly have been made, *dahling*.

It is always maliciously amusing to home in on the cutaway shots which are stuck to the screen like tacky passport photos when the nominees are read out by a visiting dinner jacket. Camera zooms in and, despite the fact that the bottom has just dropped out of the world of several hapless unfortunates, they manage anyway to produce a grin so large that it's almost as if they had just been given the secret of eternal youth. The smile is a useful symbol for deceit, Hollywood's most constant stock-in-trade.

Absence of Malice?

It was after those 1982 Academy Awards that an aggrieved film fan felt moved enough to place an ad in the pages of *Daily Variety*. It read:

To the members of the Academy: I would sincerely like you to see *The Verdict* once more and tell me what Paul Newman has to do to win an

Paul Newman, in *The Verdict*, lost many times in bid to win an Oscar.

Academy Award.
Supervisor Ed Jones
Ventura County

Newman had yet again been cheated of his due. Critically acclaimed for his role as a boozy, self-doubting lawyer, the five-times nominee was hungering for the top prize. Throughout the year staff at 20th Century-Fox had referred to *The Verdict* as Paul Newman's Academy Award movie. Newman's own view, declared to *Time* magazine, was that, 'It was such a relief to let it all hang out in the movie – blemishes and all.'

Needless to say, when the critics once again spoke sense, the Oscar decision-makers recoiled. In the *New York Times* Janet Maslin wrote: 'A solidly old-fashioned courtroom drama such as *The Verdict* could have gotten by with a serious measured performance from its leading man or it could have worked well with a dazzling movie-star turn. The fact that Paul Newman delivers both makes a clever, suspenseful, enthralling movie even better.'

Still, the Oscar flame had already scorched Newman back in 1964 when the Awards were trotted out for the past year's work, which included *Hud*. Back then the *New Yorker* was bold enough to print: 'The Academy may as well give him an Oscar right now and get it over with.'

The picture was so powerful that critics felt it could do no wrong. *Daily Variety* led the pack at an early stage: 'A picture comes along and grabs you by the throat. You sit there, spellbound. You say, "This is the way it really is." You don't merely see the picture, you live it. And when it's over, you've changed. You see life in a new way. *Hud* is such a motion picture.'

The *New York Times* expertly tapped the core of the movie: 'A drama of moral corruption – of the debilitating disease of avaricious self-seeking – that is creeping across the land and infecting the minds of young people in this complex, materialistic age.'

Bosley Crowther loved *Hud* because it seemed to him, 'a profound contemplation of the human condition'. One suspects, however, that what the mass audience most enjoyed was watching the swaggering Newman, all curling lip and arrogant stare, eat people up as an amoral Texan who, by fooling around with countless girls, causes a squeaky-clean community to break out in a collective rash. *Life* neatly summed up Newman's appeal: 'Hud is the sort of non-hero who has become Paul Newman's special province.'

The whole picture scored with glowing reviews for other performers as well. Melvyn Douglas (the pure-at-heart patriarch), Brandon de Wilde (the naïve nephew) and Patricia Neal (the housekeeper Newman tries to rape) were all allowed to bask in the critical spotlight. De Wilde, in fact, was finally the only lead from *Hud* who was not nominated for an Oscar.

And yet, despite a set of great performances, it was Newman who swamped the picture. Director Martin

Ritt was able to tap Newman's cool stare and brooding presence and employ it to not only define the behaviour of the other characters but to dominate the entire film. When his name was called up during the read-out from the podium, he received an especially warm round of applause, but no Oscar (Newman finally received an Oscar in 1986 for *Color of Money*).

The Politics of Envy

Fortunately, Steven Spielberg also has a beard to help bury his anxiety. It is quite outrageous that he is regularly cold-shouldered by Tinseltown's venerable rulers who presumably deeply resent the success which was his from the word go. He had barely left film school when, at 25, he directed *Duel* in 1971 for CBS and proved himself an edge-of-the-seat talent. Despite his untainted track record (apart from the bitsy *1941* which almost blew the bank for two studios), he has always been kept at arm's length by those who turn a deeper shade of green at the thought of his achievements.

That he has almost single-handedly brought back millions to the cinema the world over and also makes terrific movies is clearly not a prerequisite for Oscar success. Much better to dish out the golden trophy to some third-rate stodge whose director is not a threat. To boot, Spielberg is also a decent chap which is bound to boost the hatred factor against him. Now that his long-time lover and current wife Amy Irvine is about to prise his squillions from him via the divorce courts, he might just be brought more into the Hollywood fold. If, in court, he is seen to have been fooling around, or, alternatively, to be a bearded devil, he will surely be acclaimed as 'one of the boys' and so go on to reap Oscars-a-plenty.

For now, though, he is isolated by success. How could he have felt, when, sitting there watching a procession of colleagues go forward to claim their statuettes, he was completely ignored at the 1977 Academy Awards? *Close Encounters of the Third Kind* had shown itself to be a creative and commericial smash and shot Spielberg into the superleague.

Even during shooting there were rumours that *Encounters* was something special. The *New York Times* printed that the feature 'has been cloaked in almost as much secrecy as the Manhattan [atomic bomb] Project'. *Time* magazine had its foot firmly jammed in the studio door and could only come up with: 'Cast and crew have been forbidden to discuss the movie's contents in interviews – security guards have watched over its sets round the clock, at one point assiduously ejecting Spielberg when he showed up without his ID badge.'

Richard Dreyfuss, who played lead in the movie, ignored the press for some time until he finally blustered: 'If I told you anything Steve would kill me. All I can say is that in *Jaws*, the shark was the star of the film; in this film, the film is the star of the film.' Spielberg himself admitted to *American Film*: 'I didn't clamp the lid down because of egocentric reasons . . . I wanted to surprise. And the only way in the world you're going to do that is by keeping quiet about what's in it.'

Columbia's top brass leaked sweat when a journalist from *New York* magazine used bribery to glean a ticket for the film's first preview (a semi-secret low-key screening) in Dallas, and later wrote: 'I can understand all the apprehension. In my humble opinion, the picture will be a colossal flop.' The studio's cage was rattled even further when share prices dropped at once, but it gritted its teeth anyway and flew in critics from every corner of the States to meet Spielberg and his cast. They appeared sincere when they gushed: 'I want to thank you, Steven, for giving us this film' (producer Michael Phillips); and, 'I think of it as a religious film' (actress Melinda Dillon).

These US critics, and most others the world over, were next to make the intruder from *New York* a complete fool. The reviews were quite sensational, and 'masterpiece', 'creative heights' and 'Spielberg is king' littered newspaper columns around the world. Rona Barrett, normally of the 'please-me-or-forget-it' school of sensitivity, was soon frothing at both ends: 'An incredible experience,' she wrote, 'Steven Spielberg proves himself to be a consummate movie-maker and an artist of rare insight.'

Encounters simultaneously hit the cover of *Newsweek* in which Jack Kroll scribbled: '*Close Encounters* is the friendliest, warmest science-fiction epic you've ever seen. It brings the heavens down to earth.' Ray Bradbury in the *Los Angeles Times* let his enthusiasm rip: '*Close Encounters* is, in all probability, the most important film of our time.'

There was only the odd sourpuss. One of them was Rex Reed who grumbled about 'a wasteful depressing failure . . . Living in New York, I'm surrounded by enough intergalactic freaks already.' Clearly movie fans did not agree with old Rex. Queueing from day one, they have succeeded in making the film Columbia's most lucrative film to date.

With the run-up to the Oscars the fangs were out to give Spielberg a nasty bite. When it was announced that he had not even been *nominated* in the 'Best Picture' category, it was generally perceived that Steven was not the most popular kid on the block, even if he was the most talented. By being refused that nomination, he ended up in the tacky company of *Saturday Night Fever* which, although it had entertained millions, was hardly a creative first like *Encounters*.

The *Christian Science Monitor* quite rightly fumed: 'What happened to

Close Encounters of the Third Kind? Its blood brother, *Star Wars*, is lots of fun, but the picture that represents a whole year should have more heft – which is exactly what *Close Encounters* has to offer.'

Spielberg knew he would be boxing with his chum George Lucas, who had made *Star Wars*, in the 'Best Director' category, but Spielberg was clearly the better choice, since he laced his special effects with deep human experience and credible acting. As it was, *Close Encounters* was embarrassingly absent from the most prestigious categories but did manage to score a first for 'Best Cinematography', and secured a begrudging additional prize for sound effects editing.

By 1982 it seemed as if *ET* might finally fly the flag for Spielberg at that year's Academy Awards. With great reviews, it also broke all existing box-office records from day one and did in fact manage to collect nine nominations. Rex Reed got it right this time when he wrote back from the Cannes Film Festival, trumpeting that Spielberg 'showed the Godards and the Antonionis and the Fassbinders who had bored everyone into a state of catatonia for the previous two weeks how real movies are made'. Sheila Benson of the *Los Angeles Times* made even Reed's proclamation seem shy by comparison: 'It may be the film of the decade and possibly the double decade.' Even the *New Yorker*'s notorious Pauline Kael enthused that it was 'a dream of a movie – a bliss out'.

'ET phone home' was the year's catch phrase. It adorned bumper stickers, political cartoons and entered conversations all over the world. Neil Diamond was so moved that he recorded 'Turn on Your Heart Light' which tweaked the collective American heartstrings and became a must for weddings and bar mitzvahs. After Spielberg licensed more than 50 entrepreneurs to sell ET to the universe, the billions rolled in.

But on Awards night *ET* was soundly trounced by *Gandhi*, Sir Richard Attenborough's eulogy on a great man. Attenborough is typical of the kind of dull British director who can turn sparkling material into a routine exercise. Hamstrung by its theatrical approach, *Gandhi* was a linear plod which threw up one damn experience after another. Praised for months in advance because of its respectably serious subject-matter, and with Attenborough blabbing on to countless journalists, it was the ideal film to expose Hollywood's hypocrisy. It so often turns its back on the populist pictures which earn the millions required to keep the whole industry afloat and instead opts for decent-but-dull arthouse fodder so as to tart up its tarnished credibility.

Vincent Canby of the *New York Times* was furious: '*ET* and *Tootsie* are films. *Gandhi* is a laboriously illustrated textbook.' His colleague Janet Maslin agreed: 'Someday, the sweep that brought *Gandhi* eight Awards may be known as one of the great injustices in the annals of Oscardom.'

Spielberg, nice guy that he is, sat on his pride though it must have been difficult. Trying to joke around, he said, 'Look we tried our best. We stuffed the ballot boxes, we just didn't stuff them enough.' To the *Los Angeles Times* he said, 'We were almost precluded from awards because people feel we've already been amply rewarded . . . The tendency is for important films to win over popcorn entertainment. History is more weighty than popcorn.'

Who's Afraid of Richard Burton?

Richard Burton was another to find himself cheated by the suits who run the Academy. Before the 1970 Awards, at which he was up for 'Best Actor' for *Anne of the Thousand Days*, he quipped: 'Oh, I suppose 30 years from now Peter O'Toole and I will still be appearing on talk shows plugging for our first Oscar.' This, the fourth nomination for Peter O'Toole, for *Goodbye Mr Chips*, was already Burton's fifth.

Elizabeth Taylor, not surprisingly, indicated where her preference for the Award lay: 'We want Richard to win an Oscar,' she exclaimed. 'I've won an Award, Richard never has you know.'

Unlike the 1966 ceremony where Burton and Taylor were nominated for *Who's Afraid of Virginia Woolf* (she won), they decided to attend this time round. Indeed Liz explained to CBS that she regretted that her husband had not won for *Virginia Woolf*, since she considered it 'his greatest performance because the weak character is so unlike him'.

Newspaper stories at the time revolved around Liz's intention to wear the $1.5 million diamond necklace which Burton had given her. Yet even it was upstaged by Taylor as she failed to mask her disappointment when Burton fell at the final hurdle.

Their desolation could not have been helped by John Wayne who scooped first prize for *True Grit*. Backstage, he told a reporter from the *Oklahoma City Oklahoman* the following: 'It's ironic that I got the Oscar for a role that was the easiest of my career. I just hippity-hopped through it.'

Oscar's Origins

Perhaps the greatest Oscar scandal of all concerns the reason for the Academy's existence in the first place.

In 1926 Hollywood was a film-factory and Louis B. Mayer, the snarling despot at Metro-Goldwyn-Mayer, was the biggest of the studio barons. Keen to keep power confined to a few hands, preferably his own, he founded the Academy as a means of thwarting the unions which studio craftsmen were queueing up to join.

Things reached a pretty pass when Louis B. instructed the studio art director to build him a brand new house. He spat fire when he learnt that unionized studio labour would be unsuitable since it cost way too much. Enter Louis with big muscles and hefty jackboots.

Over Sunday dinner at his now-finished Santa Monica beach house, he concocted a body which would mediate labour disputes, give a PR gloss to the entire film industry and also be an élite club which would stage yearly banquets. When he snuck in his two lawyers, Edwin Loeb and George W. Cohen (known as 'the father of motion-picture contracts'), Louis's charitable intentions were plain as pie.

To read Hollywood is to be master of the sub-plot. When next you see a glossy, tanned star thanking his mother for having the foresight to give birth to him, just think that the expensive party which gives out the Academy Awards was an attempt to squash the slaves who built Hollywood. Under every smile a scandal.

Till DEATH, LUST or CASH Do Us Part

'Where's the Rest of Me?'

What about the blissful twinning of old gunslinger Ronnie with Jane Wyman? Hedda and Louella and all Hollywood had them marked as the most together couple in town. Certainly it was not only impossible to imagine them having sex outside of their marriage, or perhaps even within it, but it also seemed unlikely that they ever even had rows about who would put the cat out at night.

So their 1949 divorce shook whatever grip morality still exerted on Tinseltown. Rattled to the back teeth, onlookers soon realized that hard-headed jealousy and biting resentment were the cause. In 1948 Reagan admitted to Hedda Hopper: 'If this comes to a divorce I think I'll name *Johnny Belinda* co-respondent.' This was the 1948 film in which Wyman was such a knockout as a deaf-mute that she scooped up an Oscar at a time when Ronnie, whose acting style consisted of pointing his suit at the camera, was almost disappearing from sight. (It was his ultimate screen triumph as President which would restore his fortunes in later years.) In the months following Wyman's Oscar success, the cute couple were out for dinner one evening. The waiter, with sarcastically raised eyebrows, asked: 'And what will *Mr* Wyman have?'

The only 3-D performance which Reagan managed to squeeze from his cardboard character was his role as amputee Drake McHugh in *King's Row*, directed by Sam Wood in 1942. Upon waking up after losing both his

Ronald Reagan and Jane Wyman, famous Hollywood divorcees.

legs in an altercation with a train, the future President of the US uttered the immortal words: 'Where's the rest of me?' Savouring it as his best performance, Ronnie modestly screened it to guest after guest at his dinner parties. When the marriage was crumbling into tiny pieces, Jane said to a friend, 'I just couldn't watch that damned *King's Row* anymore.' In the divorce courts she tactfully referred to his new fascination with politics as the main reason.

However, Reagan was not one to give a tarnished image much elbow room. Proving even at this early stage that he had the non-stick quality which kept dirt at a distance, he met his present wife Nancy Davis (born Anne Frances Robbins) and soon swung back onto the track of decency. They first met when gleaming Ron was the liberal president of the Screen Actors' Guild and Nancy was a true-blue who was ridiculously suspected of Commie connections. More daft a link is difficult to imagine. Taking her out to dinner to indicate that they had pointed the finger at the wrong Nancy Davis, Ron got heavily involved with a woman who, in *The Next Voice You Hear*, heard the voice of God on the radio. She married Reagan in 1953.

Nancy certainly seems to have squeezed any namby-pamby liberal tendencies out of her husband. A reasonable Democrat in an earlier life, he now fired off broadsides against homosexuals (as Governor of California, he fired two of his staff for being gay) and indulged in right-wing knee-jerking to such an extent that he was fired as a TV presenter from 'General Electric Theater'.

Ronnie seems to have been a toy in Nancy's hands. Her surgeon stepfather was said to have been 'intolerant of minorities'. To the astonishment of the press hacks at a Chicago fundraiser in 1980, she gushed to her hubby over an amplified phone line that she wished he could be there to 'see all these beautiful white people'.

In Like Clint

Just as solid as Ron and Nance were Clint and Maggie Eastwood. Despite the queue of lovelies present on any film lot for a hoped-for fling with Dirty Harry, the chin himself was seemingly devoted to Maggie and the two kids. He would go to any lengths to protect them from press snooping.

Sondra Locke, to whom Clint is now wedded, first popped up to act in *The Outlaw Josey Wales* in 1976, after which she returned to face Clint in *The Gauntlet*. The crew noticed the closeness of the couple and notions of a romance were paraded in print when they turned up for the première of a film called *First Love*. It was generally felt that they were having a close encounter of the first kind.

It was agent William Morris who

jammed his foot firmly in his mouth when he said: 'We understand Clint is looking for a script as a basis for another movie in which Miss Sondra Locke will star. He will perhaps both direct and act opposite her in any new film.'

From this point on Sondra was never off the screen. *Every Which Way But Loose* in 1978 led to *Any Which Way You Can* and *Bronco Billy*, both in 1980. For a man who claims to shun the limelight, it was a mite foolish to take Sondra along to a celebrity motor race after which Miss Locke clumsily exclaimed: 'Everybody would love for us to say, "Its all true, we are madly in love." But people will believe whatever they want to believe. Even if it was true – which it isn't – I certainly would not talk about it.'

Maggie must have felt like an island. She had clung to Clint during the TV series 'Rawhide', including the time when it was temporarily cancelled, and backed him in his decision to make *A Fistful of Dollars*, the first of the 'Spaghetti Westerns' in 1964, when others advised against it.

She also had a relaxed attitude towards his celebrity status. Once, when sitting outside an Italian café, Clint was asked to pose with a beautiful Oriental model. Soon the picture appeared with the caption: 'Could this love affair end in marriage?' Maggie was good at laughing all this off.

Clint once talked to a journalist about other women: 'I guess Maggie understands these are the hazards of my business, but Maggie is a very smart lady. I respect her and her opinions, although we don't always agree.'

To another he let a small but significant cat out of the bag: 'Maggie doesn't own me. The worst thing is *owning* people. I don't want to own *anybody*; shared maybe, but not owned lock, stock and barrel.'

He continued: 'To me love for a person is respect for feelings. Love is respecting privacy, accepting faults, but I don't believe its a one-way street. The sophisticated woman accepts that the chances are a guy's not being 100 per cent faithful.'

Exit Clint from his $3 million house, leaving Maggie with Kyle, ten, and Alison, six. After deciding to kick Clint down the garden path for good, she has since emerged to successfully claim his millions.

In topsy-turvy Tinseltown, where suburbanites are really sex fiends, and half-baked actors later come out of hiding to run the world, it comes as no surprise to find that marriage is often shown the door along with honesty, decency, trust and other interfering virtues.

The Snake Charmer

The elegantly named Lionel Atwill, cinema's best early mad doctor, had a life which on the surface seemed the first and last word in civilization. In reality, however, it churned away like the gothic nightmare world of his films. Everyone in movieland was astonished that this clean-cut firmjaw was a twisted creep who abused women like throwaway souvenirs and hosted rollercoaster sex sessions in the afternoons to which he invited his friends. He considered marriage to be no more than a passing fad which lasted until his loins began to give and his appetite to stray. He is now primarily a symbol of all the lurid naughtiness which the world has come to expect of Hollywood.

Atwill himself tellingly remarked: 'See – one side of my face is gentle and kind, incapable of anything but love of my fellow-man. The other side, the other profile, is cruel and predatory and evil, incapable of anything but the lusts and dark passions. It all depends which side of my face is turned toward you – or the camera. It all depends which side faces the moon at the ebb of the tide.'

The devil and the angel who played tricks with his face also used his screen persona to transfix the public. Atwill was a master at exploiting his plummy open-vowelled British baritone to speak exquisitely about sinister irrational fears and man's darkest experiences. It's a bit like a perfectly modulated Oxbridge graduate calmly announcing that we're all going to be nuked in five minutes.

Could this smooth-chinned Englishman, who invested in art after each successful picture (e.g. Sir Henry Raeburn's 'Lady with a Shawl' after his success in *Doctor X*) also be the slavering host who showed hours of porno pics to his filthy friends and allowed a teenage flirt from Minnesota to invite his chums in for a good time until she was carrying a passenger? The public thought, impossible, but we now know better.

On the outside a model of suburban virtue, he was born to wealthy Croydon parents who unsuccessfully tried to steer him towards architecture. Quickly becoming a leading man in London's West End, he was first invited to the States by the legendary Lillie Langtry, Edward VII's favourite pin-up.

His career quickly took root in America where two of his earliest roles seemed tailor-made for his black make-up: *The Lodger in New York* saw him hit the spotlight as a Jack the Ripper-style fruitcake, while in *Another Man's Shoes* (1922) he popped up as a fellow with a split personality, truly ensuring he had no rehearsing to do whatsoever.

His first marriage ended, surprisingly not through sweaty antics on dirty Lionel's part, but through a spot of the horizontal on his wife's. Mrs Atwill (the actress Elsie McKay) was indulging herself with one Max Montesole (amusingly a protégé of Lionel's) when Atwill and the cops burst in in true camp-movie style. It was 1928 and Atwill promptly secured a divorce.

Within what seemed like minutes he tied the knot with Louise Cromwell, a direct descendant of Oliver Cromwell. Louise was an heiress with a handy stash, who had recently ditched Douglas MacArthur, the hulk who would be General.

1931 was to send Atwill on a sharp upward climb. In that year Universal had coined it with *Dracula* and *Frankenstein*. Warners shrewdly realized that naked horror was just the ticket for scaring the Depression-era masses and so let loose full-frontal fear to take their minds off their next meal, which could easily be a couple of days off.

The studio thus brought out *Doctor X* in 1932, a film which was a treat for Lionel's splintered persona. With eyes 'like Satanic neons', according to film historian William Everson, he seemed to revel in a picture which threw up rape, cannibalism, dismemberment, necrophilia, as well as a kinky scene where nasty Li receives a brief sexual thrill on seeing Preston Foster unscrewing his false arm.

Next up was *The Mystery of the Wax Museum* (1933) in which Atwill hogs the screen as a crazy sculptor whose face is smacked hard by Fay Wray. The mask crumbles and a horrid monster is revealed underneath. Still in 1933, his medical charms fill the frame again in *The Vampire Bat*, while in *Murders in the Zoo* he employs a tasty range of killer animals to dispose of his wife's lovers. In this latter film Li stalks the jungle where he leaves an unfortunate fellow to be eaten by beasts after first sewing up his lips.

Just remember that this high-octane demon was going home at night to a properly turned out wife in a nice neighbourhood. Atwill's non-stop hits had enabled him to buy a Spanish-style sprawl in the top-drawer suburb of Pacific Palisades where mock-Tudor cottages hold hands with plenty of prim churches and manners ruleth over all. The plush property had been found for Lionel and Louise by James Whale, who had directed our friend in *One More River* (1934) (where he plays the lawyer of a warped husband). Whale himself went on to hit the spotlight as a single-minded aficionado of young boys. For a short time the local Boy Scouts played a leading role.

On the surface the marriage was relaxed and successful. Armed with breeding and social poise, Louise had a brother who became Ambassador to Canada. Such graciousness combined formidably with her husband's movie successes and so enabled them to be regular dinner guests of William Randolph Hearst and Marion Davies. After her father's death, Louise's mother continued to move up the social ladder and landed Edward Stotesbury, big-time money-man and art collector. Old Stotesbury had given Louise a nice 'little present' when she married MacArthur: a vast Georgian residence in the heart of Maryland.

After leaving MacArthur, she was now to dump Lionel. Eventually the reasons for the Atwills' split were teased out. Lionel's kinky habits often led to the comforting presence of a chambermaid or chauffeur in the marital bed. As far as we know, Louise had no objection to this and may well have actually enjoyed the triangular romps. She did, however, draw the line at a snake. Obviously attractive for a man who wallowed in the ambiguous arena of sex and danger (one of his great thrills in between filming was sitting in on murder trials), Lionel became a massive fan of Elsie, his co-star in *Murders in the Zoo*. Elsie was the total kink, a 15 ft (4.5 m) python which smutty Atwill tried to introduce to the marital bed. At this Louise responded in a spirit of true meanness and threatened to leave her husband.

Atwill had once told a journalist: 'All women love the men they fear. All women kiss the hand that rules them. . . Women are cat creatures. Their preference is for a soft fireside cushion, for delicate bowls of cream, for perfumed leisure and for a *master*!'

Strange to relate, Louise did not fall in with her husband's profound, far-seeing and truly relaxed view of marriage and walked out forever, euphemistically blaming events on Atwill's 'surly character'. She did, in fact, end up in Washington where she hosted a radio show called 'Mrs Atwill's Dinner Party' in which she lampooned leading political figures.

With a sex drive on the loose and only a macaw, Elsie and six Dalmatians (all regular bed-guests) for company, frisky Li turned his home into a mad sex parlour to which friends like directors Josef von Sternberg and Eddie Goulding were regularly invited. These no-clothes shenanigans were to end Atwill in court.

Atwill insisted on certain standards at his fun parties. He ensured that all guests were not just up to physical scratch but also had a predilection for the role-playing and imaginative sex of which Lionel himself was so truly fond. On top of this he wanted his guests to be clean of body, if not spirit, and so he packed them all off for regular VD checks.

All this could only remain quiet for so long and consequently, in December 1940, two floozies began to spew the truth. A tale unwound about Sylvia, a fresh-faced sixteen-year-old dairy queen from the Mid-West, who had been morally twisted by Lionel's parties at which the centrepiece had been much strenuous activity on a tiger-skin rug. Lionel objected in court that his rug was in fact bearskin not tiger. The two tarts said that Li's saucy movies included *The Plumber and the Girl* and *The Daisy Chain*, with Atwill protesting under oath that the only films he owned were 'travelogues and short subjects dealing with home life in many lands'. Newspapers had a terrific time comparing Lionel to a Svengali figure whose parties upstaged the naughty nooky of ancient Rome.

A second star-turn in court landed Atwill five years' probation for perjury, before he was finally let off the hook for good after seven months, since the accuser 'was not actuated by a sincere desire to bring about justice'.

Louise's divorce from her husband finally came through in 1943, the result of which was a sizeable property settlement. Revelations in court about dirty Li had also had a sharp spin-off on her. While stories about tiger-skin (or bearskin) rugs and 15 ft pythons were shocking a jury and entrancing a public (who now realized that sex was no longer just five minutes of missionary on a marital bed), she received a stream of poison letters from all-American puritans who believed that, if she was capable of ditching the wholesome MacArthur for a part-time mad doctor and full-time sex maniac, then she ought to string herself up. Louise ignored the suggestion but was heard to whisper to big-shot friends in Washington that, if she really dumped on not only Atwill, but MacArthur as well, 'it would shake some circles harder than the earthquake in Alaska'. Still, well-bred to the last, Louise never turned her private whisperings into public shoutings.

Although smiled upon by the law, Atwill was now shunted off set by Hollywood which now regarded him as a wholesale pervert rather than one of their most successful actors. He ended up making low-budget quickies which were shot in a matter of days. His pathetic demise was no match for his full-blast lifestyle; while filming *Lost City of the Jungle* in 1946, he folded up with pneumonia and a double was wheeled on to complete his scenes.

Atwill, of course, was the proof par excellence that things ain't never what they seem, especially in Hollywood where the big screen image and sycophantic gossip-writers have cloaked the gods we have worshipped in a warmly deceptive sheen.

MONEY FOR NOTHING

Grasping paws are nothing new in Hollywood. In the wake of the enormous power which now landed in the lap of the new upstart movie barons came the flood of filthy lucre which magnetized these one-time paupers from the east coast streets. Rip-offs are such an integral part of the status quo that they are often taken for granted or completely ignored. If the powerful and pushy started behaving with thoughtfulness and decency and stopped dipping their snouts in the trough, then the entire Hollywood community would reel from shock and imagine it had been transported to Mars.

Time of Corruption

In a recent edition of the august *New York Times*, three of its best reporters commented on the far-reaching nature of corruption. Robert Lindsey, Jeff Gerth and Aljean Harmetz wrote of 'a pattern of questionable financial

Cliff Robertson, innocently involved in forged cheque scandal.

practices throughout the motion picture industry. According to Columbia and law enforcement sources, the film business is permeated by financial irregularities that extend from the executive suite to the movie backlot to the local theater box office. . .'

It was Richard Brooks, the Academy Award-winning writer and director who said ten years ago: 'Nobody can skim as well as Las Vegas because they invented it. But Hollywood is second. It's a time of corruption.'

Brooks's utterances came in the aftermath of the greatest Hollywood financial scandal in years, that of David Begelman and the forged cheques in 1978. This had such an unsettling effect throughout the entire industry that it has seen executives clinging to their cashmere coats with guilt and actors looking at them sideways even more than before.

The long and complex saga which was to unseat Begelman (then president of Columbia) began with an everyday meeting between actor Cliff Robertson (best known for his 1976 lead role in *Obsession*) and his secretary Evelyn Christel who arrived at the Robertson residence on 25 February 1977 to leaf through the day's correspondence.

Robertson, whose strict Presbyterian upbringing made him a stickler for right and wrong, was already scoffed at in Hollywood because he led a satisfying family life and didn't *need* the industry. In amongst the usual correspondence was a tax statement which claimed that Robertson had received a cheque the previous year for $10,000 and would he be so kind as to cough up the tax on it. Seeing that Cliff had done no work for Columbia during this period, it struck him as just slightly odd.

As gestures of good will from the studios, actors and directors are often paid lump sums on an ad hoc basis so that loyalty and cordial relations can be maintained. It is not unusual, for example, for a director to be given a spanking new limousine at the end of a shoot.

After persistent enquiries by Robertson and his secretary, Columbia claimed the $10,000 had been paid to assist Robertson on the promotional tour for *Obsession*. Clearly more than Robertson would be likely to spend in those circumstances, such a fistful comes fittingly into the 'goodwill' category. Yet Robertson had never received such a cheque so he wasn't too keen to pay tax on it.

After negotiating the complex web that is now Hollywood, Robertson eventually discovered that Begelman had forged a cheque in his name and received $10,000 in American Express travellers' cheques.

After the details of Begelman's crimes were teased out in court, it was revealed that the president of Columbia had pocketed a mere $60,000. A manic greed seemed to be driving the personality of a man who had been earning an easy third of a million dollars per year.

Just when Begelman was being

traumatized by current complainants, up popped the spectre of Sid Luft who thought the time was ripe to revive a lawsuit. The ex-husband of Judy Garland, he had filed a suit against Begelman in 1966, accusing him of writing phoney cheques on his wife's account.

Luft's suspicion of Begelman went back as far as 1961 when Garland hired Begelman (then an agent) to manage her affairs. It was two years later when Luft regained control of his wife's career that he and his accountant found discrepancies in the books.

First off were 13 cheques for $36,000 which Begelman had forged in Garland's name and cashed in at different Las Vegas hotels. Next to flee Miss Garland's cosy nestegg was the tidy sum of $50,000 which sped its way from a Garland account in London to a mystery account in New York. Guess whose? Then, by what must surely have been an error of bureaucracy, a further $10,000 was switched from an account, which honest Dave held in trust for Garland, to an account in his own name.

Finally, there was the matter of an expensive Cadillac which Judy should have received for her appearance on the Jack Paar TV show in 1962. Registered in the name of Begelman, it was a luxury to which Garland never even knew she was entitled! The fleecing of Judy assumes a particularly sad twist when it was revealed by two of her children, Liza Minelli and Joseph Luft, that their mother had died a virtual bankrupt.

Despite the gravity of his crimes, Begelman received only three years' probation and a $5,000 fine which is apparently appropriate for a first offender in the realm of grand theft. In sentencing Begelman, Judge Thomas Murphy graphically outlined Begelman's greed-through-innocence: 'If you had painted your hand red and let it drip on the floor you couldn't have better called your crime to anyone's attention.'

As well as being ordered into psychiatric care, he was also instructed to produce something of benefit to the community. The result was *Angel Death*, a documentary on the legal dangers of drug abuse. Perhaps a full-blown feature on the fatal attraction of hard cash would have been more suitable. Michael Douglas and *Wall Street* had yet to arrive.

Yet the startling aspect of the Begelman scandal was not simply that a millionaire would go to such grasping lengths to cheat that extra dollar from an ignorant victim but the effect these revelations had in Hollywood.

Columbia, despite being rattled to the back teeth, consoled its shareholders with the solid fact that its then current biggie, *Close Encounters of the Third Kind*, had just topped $50 million at the box office. The super-sell of toys, T-shirts and assorted trivia would be certain to placate them even more.

Fixing the Books

But elsewhere the sordid scandal caused plenty of high-profile reaction. Fraud was now revealed as a natural part of everyday life in Tinseltown: bribes to studio executives from independent producers eager to secure backing, the pocketing of money from production budgets by cash-hungry producers, not to mention the concealment of profits by distributors and the outright lies of cinema owners about the number of tickets sold.

One famous result was the filing of a suit against Allied Artists by Sean Connery and Michael Caine, who insisted loudly that the profits they were due from *The Man Who Would Be King* (1976) had never arrived in the post. After filing in a New York court, Connery explained: 'I've never stolen from anybody in my life. To work in good faith and be cheated is wrong. I'm tired of being robbed.' More courageous than most actors perhaps because he is more secure in his career and star-status, Connery was till then one of the few to have complained in public.

Now actors lined up to vent their wrath on their employers. Many complained that overheads, distribution, equipment hire, and even advertising, publicity and phone calls, were being deducted from the cost of the picture before they received their share. Robert Montgomery, a New York lawyer, commented: 'I don't think this is cheating in the criminal sense, but I do think managements take advantage of every possibility available to them.'

Next to mouth off as a result of Begelman's antics were the cinema owners who complained about the shoddy behaviour of the big studios. 20th Century-Fox ended up in court trying to fend off the accusation that they would only release the highly lucrative *Star Wars* to some cinemas provided these venues would allow themselves to be lumbered with *The Other Side of Midnight*, which was then trying to scratch a living. Marvin Goldman, president of the National Association of Theater Owners, summed up national feeling which had exploded as a result of Begelman and his paltry cheques: 'I think if our industry was held up to the light and you shook it a lot of worms would fall out.'

The Film That Sank a Studio

The other major modern financial scandal has to be the mad wastage behind the making of *Heaven's Gate* by Michael Cimino, the man who made *The Deer Hunter*. *Heaven's Gate*, released in 1980, is a film that has become synonymous with massive egos, chronic mismanagement, epic malpractice and spending sums equivalent to the annual turnover of small nations. So great was the disaster that it sank United Artists for good.

A big screen western with a production budget of $7.5 million finally cost $36 million. Decisions about the movie were being made by people who were thousands of miles apart and who were not even in regular contact. Cimino even managed to keep the film from his employers so that they were unable to see a single frame before the disastrous opening night.

One of the many blunders was that Cimino, inexplicably, had never actually signed the budget agreement. Lawyers began to pull out their hair as they tried to give some legal substance to the studio's insistence on keeping costs down. Meanwhile the maverick Cimino, whose obsessive perfectionism was an equal match for his outsize ego, was flagrantly defying orders from Hollywood.

By placing cast and crew on call and on overtime, he hoped to finish the film to meet the Christmas 1979 deadline. Instead the work schedule expanded to fill those extra hours so that, as it was later calculated, a day was lost for each day shot. Normal rates were boosted by double time and triple time on Sundays, while enough film to stretch round the planet and back was causing the Hollywood bosses to bark like mad dogs.

On the set itself there was no frenzy whatsoever as Cimino fed hundreds of thousands of feet of film into his constantly whirring cameras in an all-out attempt at perfection. Everything moved at a pace which, if any slower, would have ground proceedings to a halt. Frantic accountants had by now worked out that production costs had shot into the twilight zone and were running at over $1 million a week.

Executive Derek Kavanagh flew to Montana where the film was being shot. As well as examining the amount of screen-time shot, he also scrutinized camera and production reports and rounded up accounts paid and owing. He concluded that shooting would never be completed by Christmas and remarked too that certain local roads were to close for a time and so the schedule would be stretched even further.

Cimino, he calculated, was running through a massive two hours of film to shoot just over half a script page, which would eventually result in only 1½ minutes on the screen. For this freewheeling addiction to his art, he was burning up $200,000 a day.

Before the prologue and epilogue were added to the film, not to mention expensive post-production, the total for shooting came to $27,024,884.29. These add-ons caused the budget to sky-rocket to $44 million (now including promotional costs), a figure which seems to knowingly mock the first budget estimate of $7.5 million.

Cimino's big-headed notion of art at any price is crazy when you realize that a film is not a personal whim which is exercised in a commercial vacuum but a product which has to be made, sold and marketed like any other.

That the film was trashed by critics and ignored by the public highlights even more the foolishness at the heart of its making. Hollow laughter could be heard throughout Hollywood. Artistic holes abound in a movie which shunts credible characters and storylines aside in its mad pursuit of wide-screen effects. Cimino's obsession with detail ensured that characters were two-dimensional and left most audiences stone cold. However, since the film was re-released in a form close to its original length, it has been re-appraised by some critics. But the public still has to flock.

Burning Banknotes

The carefree spending on *Heaven's Gate* seemed to hit Hollywood like a nasty disease. *Star Trek* (1979), *The Wiz* (1978), *The Blues Brothers* (1980), *Reds* (1981), *Raise The Titanic* (1980) (which sank Lew Grade) and *1941* (1979) (with which golden boy Stephen Spielberg almost sank two studios) all notched up mad budgets of between $25–30 million.

Certain expensive failures have also been largely due to a surreal mismatch of man and material. Which studio greysuit could have possibly thought that John Schlesinger, he of *Far From the Madding Crowd* (1967) on screen and *Der Rosenkavalier* at Covent Garden, would be the perfect choice for *Honky Tonk Freeway* (1981) whose cast of loopy characters required a less straight-laced director? Or who mistakenly thought that Hugh Hudson, director of *Chariots of Fire* (1981), possessed a natural empathy for the American War of Independence and so allowed him to burn banknotes on *Revolution* (1985)? Luciano Pavarotti sang perfectly well in *Yes, Giorgio* (1982), but was risible in his attempts to carry on a screen romance, while the unfettered creativity of Roman Polanski was quite wrong for the literal-minded nature of *Pirates* (1986). All these films, which lost fortunes, were part of a new era of the colossal overspend.

This is the sort of bone-headed profligacy and idiotic tunnel vision which hits Hollywood for six. In a brief two week period during summer 1984, the top management of three studios were all shown the door, while within three years of the *Heaven's Gate* free-for-all the same switch had occurred in every major Hollywood production company. It only takes a self-serving director on a set, with an ego larger than the budget available for his entire production, or a smooth-talking executive who fancies a spot of extra cash, to cause thunderbolts throughout an industry which is just learning to walk again.

Harry Cohn, standing, movie mogul who was also a 'monster'.

The cigar-chomping chin-jutting mogul is a favourite image of Hollywood which has been diluted to the level of strip cartoon. Stand-up comics both here and in America, as well as our own Goons and Pythons, have relished acting out the universally accepted caricature of the barking studio head who acts on whim and impulse and fires people he doesn't even employ.

Yet those comic creations sprang originally from a close-knit batch of Hollywood bosses whose obsessive spite and malice caused them to break employees or competitors into tiny pieces.

Joseph Patrick Kennedy hid much beneath the schoolboy grin and rogue-Irish charm. Later to bathe in the reflected glory of his gleaming family, it seems almost impossible to believe that he was possessed of a streak so harsh that he could box men into a corner so they could scarcely breath.

Harry the Hustler

An obsession with movie-making certainly kept hell-fire tactics in their place. A telling encounter between a writer and Harry Cohn, who ruled Columbia Pictures, speaks volumes:

'Whaddaya been doing?' Cohn asked the writer, whom he had not seen in some time.

'I've been in retirement writing a book,' answered the writer.

'Is there a picture in it?' demanded Cohn.

'No, I don't think so.'

'Too bad,' ended Cohn, 'I'd like to have read it.'

The business clout, Jewish wit, dismissive manner and obsession with movies is the substance of a conversation which could have been held between young writer and any one of the maverick studio bosses.

Harry Cohn, the most savage of dictators, was named 'White Fang' by writer Ben Hecht. Jewish by birth and of mixed German-Russian parentage, he seemed keener than the others to squash his roots to the point where he often sounded anti-Semitic. Once at a large party which he was hosting for studio staff, he commented on the mass rush to the buffet table, by spitting out disparagingly, 'Look at those Jews eat.'

As a youngster in New York City, he had shifted around as a pool hustler, song plugger and trolley bus driver. In his driving job he was so adept at creaming the takings that his bosses always told him that they were glad he had the decency to bring the bus back at night.

From the early 1920s to the late 1950s Cohn ran an empire which produced *It Happened One Night* (1934), *All the King's Men* (1949), *From Here to Eternity* (1953) and *The Bridge On The River Kwai* (1957). Yet his workaholic employees who made these films possible knew the darker meaning of Cohn's maxim: 'He who eats my bread sings my song.'

Cohn had been trying for a long time to lure a bright, thoughtful and sensitive young chap to Columbia. When the twin weapons of persuasion and charm failed – and Cohn could easily summon up charm at will – dollars and power were offered up instead. When appointed as an executive producer with a hefty bank balance, the young fellow at once set to work on a script with two writers. Cohn himself offered a batch of ideas which were rejected by the creative threesome. The new arrival complained to Cohn that the vote was three to one in their favour. 'You're wrong,' explained Cohn, 'it's one to nothing.'

Cohn fired the two writers immediately and from that day on reserved his meanest remarks for the producer. Over dinner in the corporate dining room he would turn to the young man with the abusive question, 'All right, Jewboy, what do you think?', while on one memorable occasion, as a number of Columbia big-shots were about to shoot off to a preview, he smiled at his victim with the remark – 'Who do you think your wife's fucking tonight?' Shortly after this the put-upon employee fled Cohn and his venom.

At press conferences to announce a new film, Cohn constantly referred to the male and female leads as 'the prick and the cunt'. Plenty of written evidence quotes Cohn as remarking, 'This time the prick will be played by . . . and the cunt by. . .'

Even his own family was not spared. On one occasion, when Sam Goldwyn and his wife came to dinner, Cohn received a call which caused him to break out in the most vulgar expletives. This coincided with one of his sons coming downstairs to wish his parents goodnight. Goldwyn, himself a hated studio head, butted in: 'Harry, you shouldn't talk like that in front of the boy. It's not right.'

'It's time he learned,' snapped Cohn and continued breathing foul abuse down the phone.

Unsurprisingly, Cohn became a major fan of Benito Mussolini after making a documentary on him so he went to visit the dictator in Italy. He loved the complex web of corridors which led to his office as well as the raised circular desk which lent Il Duce the proper pomposity. On his return to Hollywood, Cohn modelled his own office after it, refusing, like Mussolini, to take Novocaine for pain and kept the despot's photograph on his desk until he became unpopular.

As super-salesmen for the concept of the Free World through screens across the world, the most powerful men in showbusiness were in fact practising a tyranny which so many new immigrants had fled in the old world and which had no place in countless film versions of the American Dream.

'He Bit Me on the Breast'

One story in particular shows his poisonous drive. It centres on the supposed encounter between one Eunice Pringle, a teenage waster who dreamed of neon lights, and Alexander Pantages, an energetic entrepreneur who owned the Hollywood Pantages, the first really impressive art deco cinema. The theatre, in fact, lives on even now as a convenient stop-off for touring Broadway musicals. He also ran a less grandiose cinema in downtown Los Angeles. It was here that Pringle collapsed into noisy hysterics after her supposed rape by Pantages.

A cinema employee was startled to witness the plump Eunice, wrapped in a revealing red dress, running terrified from the caretaker's broom cupboard. With shrieks-a-plenty which could easily be heard by the audience above the soundtrack of the movie they were watching, she pointed accusingly at a respectable-looking, well-groomed man who was in his office next to the broom cupboard. It was, of course, Pantages. The panicky Pantages declared himself innocent to a traffic policeman who had by now been called in to investigate.

Pantages was an immigrant from Athens who splendidly exemplified the American Dream. Having sold papers and shone shoes, he vanished to Alaska during the Klondike gold strike and returned with a stash of gold nuggets. He bought his first theatre, a vaudeville venue in Seattle and, with his flair for energetic promotion, kept the public flooding in. Adding films to the bill, he soon built up his collection to 60 theatres which stretched from Canada to Mexico. By 1929 Pantages had amassed a fortune of $30 million.

However, in court his gruff, broken English did not appeal to the jury who by now had been fed constant descriptions of Eunice as 'the sweetest seventeen since Clara Bow' (*Herald-Examiner*), and 'a full-blown beauty' (*Los Angeles Times*).

To bolster the effect she turned up in court wearing a girlish frock of which Mary Pickford would have been proud and the kind of flat shoes which hardly suggest temptation. Claiming that she had gone to the cinema to show Pantages a new act she had developed, she then proceeded to intricately detail the encounter in the broom cupboard.

'He said he wanted me for his sweetheart. I told him I was not interested in sweethearts. I was interested in work, but he continued his advances. He seemed to go crazy. He clapped his hand over my mouth – he bit me on the breast.' Fainting immediately, she came round to find her dress hoisted and Pantages' privates on parade. With her girlish air and home-spun clothing, how could the jury resist Eunice? They could not.

Despite Pantages' protestations that with sex being freely available throughout movieland, he had no need to resort to rape in a broom cupboard, and despite noisy rumours that Eunice's agent was a sharp practitioner who had used her as part of some scam, Pantages was sent down for 50 years.

A timely first which was to leave an indelible mark on the law courts also served to help Pantages. His lawyer, Jerry Geisler, succeeded in gaining permission for the morals of a minor to be held up for inspection in court. Waving his evidence in front of the California Supreme Court, Geisler secured a re-trial for 1931. Declaring that 'the testimony of the prosecutrix was so improbable as to challenge credulity' and watching Geisler and Ehrlich, his associate, enact the supposed rape in court, they concluded that the assault described by Eunice would have been impossible in a broom cupboard.

An old lady who managed the Moonbeam Glen Bungalow Court, where Pringle and her devious agent had lived as man and wife, was wheeled on as an eleventh hour witness. Not particularly willing to help Pantages, she was confronted by extensive Bible readings from Ehrlich who convinced her of her moral duty. She singled out the conniving Eunice as a tenant and so Pantages finally savoured justice.

This is where the beaming Joe Kennedy comes in. Kennedy acquired RKO through his movie company FBO. RKO was quick to devour the Orpheum cinema circuit whose only rival on the West Coast was, surprise surprise, Pantages. Eunice finally confessed on her deathbed in the manner of gripping Hollywood melodrama that it was mogul Joe, the father of a future president, who had secured Eunice's compliance in the stitch-up so that Pantages would become an immediate nonentity and leave his cinema chain up for grabs. However, thanks to the maverick efforts of Jerry Geisler, who now leapt from backroom lawyer to the grand heights of 'Lawyer to the Stars', Kennedy's scheme never got off the starting block. Although this seedy incident squashed his ambitions as a big-shot movie-man, it did not deter him from quickly entering the equally morally ambiguous arena of national politics.

A neat irony completes the story. With Kennedy shunted aside, Warner Brothers took over the theatre where the incident occurred and later screened all the movies by Errol Flynn. It was the legal breakthrough which Geisler achieved that was of direct help to Flynn when he was maliciously accused of rape by two underage girls.

Hollywood Schmollywood

This sly scheme of Kennedy's seems the last word in civilized behaviour when compared to the rough-shod tactics of the other upstart moguls. Eastern European cities like Warsaw, Kiev and Minsk had propelled towards America a new generation of the ambitious and determined who were street-hustlers first and English-speakers last. Mostly Jewish, they were quick to shorn themselves of long-winded surnames and assume instead names more palatable to a homogenized community. Mayer, Warner, Zukor and Selznick were the result. Their collective rise from back-street to boardroom was a strong feature in helping to create the all-pervasive idea of the American Dream.

Between them the future dinosaurs were glove salesmen, furriers, pool hustlers and rag-and-bone men before finding a common bond in the world of nickelodeons. (These devices willed the customer to part with a few cents and delivered in return a peepshow, one's fortune or weight.) They firmly joined hands to jump into the untested waters of the movie business. Determined not to catch a cold, and ignoring criticism of the corrupting nature of film and how it could leave the viewer with a permanently strange squint, they, as immigrants, were quick to divine the appeal of a medium which could crash through class, race and language barriers.

There was also the simple paradox that these Jewish pragmatists were selling Gentile features and customs across the planet. The cute blonde hair and demure manners of Mary Pickford were a perfect match for their intentions. When Jesse Lasky of Paramount was rushed to hospital with a heart attack, he hastily replied 'American' to a simple question about race. The young Jewish official said, 'Now, now, Mr Lasky. We are Jewish aren't we?'

'Jewish, oh yes, yes, Jewish,' stuttered the surprised Lasky. These moguls, as capable of creative salesmanship as of whimsical cruelty, were paid a twisted compliment by Joseph Stalin who complained that if he could only control the film industry he could control the world.

Warner Brothers were one of the great dynasties. Sam, Albert, Harry and Jack were the four brothers. Sam, by far the most likeable, had pioneered the use of sound in *The Jazz Singer* but unfortunately died the day after it opened on 6 October 1927. It was Albert, in his capacity as Treasurer who, like our own David Puttnam, spouted fire over the stars' vast pay cheques, while Harry displayed plenty of entrepreneurial flair. He was once described by Jack as having 'the toughness of a brothel madam and the buzzing persistence of a mosquito on a hot night'. Jack was head of production and so became the best known of the famous four. He was the would-be actor who actually sang illustrated songs in his very first Warner cinema.

Busby Bugs Out

Busby Berkeley had a head-on collision with their persistence and tyranny. The outstanding director of the Hollywood musical, and the only one whose name is a dictionary entry (slang for 'a very elaborate musical number'), Berkeley's passion for his craft was matched only by his love for his mother. With five marriages on the rocks, his devotion to his mum never waned.

His dance sequences for Darryl Zanuck's *42nd Street* (1933) turned the film into a landmark as well as a means by which Warners shot out of the red. On 8 September 1935 Buzz attended a party hosted by William Koenig, the production manager at Warners, to celebrate the completion of *In Caliente*. By the time he left the party he was certainly unfit to take the wheel of his white sports car but did so anyway. In addition, he had already been burning his manic creativity on five films that year (in less than nine months) and so was weighed down by the kind of nervous exhaustion where the body demands rest but the mind keeps churning out dance numbers. Careering down the dark and twisting Pacific Coast Highway, he ended up on the wrong side of the road where he smashed into one car before killing three passengers in a second: William von Brieson, his mother Ada and his sister-in-law, Dorothy Daley. Buzz was immediately charged with second degree murder.

Now the dehumanized wallop of the Warner gang comes into its own. The helpless plight of Berkeley was a mere trifle when compared to the fact that the genius was locked into a three-picture deal for Warners which meant a bruising workload and back-to-back shooting. Big heart that he was, Jack Warner thoughtfully arranged all Berkeley's shooting schedules for nights only, seeing as he was tied up in court during the day. That Buzz had accumulated head and leg injuries and was burdened with all-out fatigue which might just benefit from sleep was never an issue for Jack Warner.

While everyone else arrived at the court-house by car, lucky Buzz came by ambulance and made daily show-stopping appearances in court on a wheeled stretcher. To this day there are some striking pictures of his testimony from the horizontal, his head wrapped in bandages. The Invisible Man would be green with envy.

Jerry Geisler, who had defended Pantages so well and was now the star's favourite (Chaplin, Flynn, Mitchum, *et al*), was commissioned by Warners to defend their dance man. He ably stacked up evidence in Berkeley's favour. A blown-out left front tyre from the white sports car was exhibited as the cause of the accident, while a battery of party guests soundly asserted that Buzz was the picture of sobriety when he left the party. They also all happened to be contracted to Warners. Still, with the star theatrics of Frank McHugh, Pat O'Brien, Glenda Farrell and Mervyn Leroy, what could a poor jury do? Acquit him, of course. This they finally did after a third trial in September 1936.

That Buzz didn't finally froth his way into an asylum was due more to the incidental effect of hard work than any strange act of kindness from the Warner despots. With creative adrenalin keeping him up all night working on *Stage Struck* (1936), he had to quickly freshen up to be in court by 9.00 a.m. each day. He commented at the time: 'Even though I was found innocent, it was a shocking and depressing thing to have been involved in the death of three people. I was lucky that I had so much work – it probably saved my sanity.'

It was extraordinary that Jack Warner's petty-minded manipulations, so often shot through with malevolence, left space in the same personality for the inventive and humanitarian impulse responsible for *The Jazz Singer* (1927), *Yanky Doodle Dandy* (1942), *My Fair Lady* (1964) and *Who's Afraid of Virginia Woolf?* (1966).

THE BOYS IN THE BAND

Rock's Pillow Talk

That same discrepancy between an image dreamed up by Hollywood and a quite different reality is relevant to the life of Rock Hudson.

For more than 30 years Hudson was the leading torch-bearer for all-American masculinity. One of the biggest screen heroes of this century, he sported a 6 ft 4 in (193 cm) frame, clean-cut looks and a healthy natural manner which appealed enormously to millions of women fans.

He placed a seal on his masculinity when, in 1956, he played opposite Elizabeth Taylor in *Giant*, a film which brought him a 'Best Actor' Oscar nomination. He then proceeded to make three pictures with Doris Day in the late 1950s and early 1960s in which he established a new trend of sexy sophistication. Even 20 years later Rock was still able to trot out his masculine charm when he starred opposite Linda Evans in 'Dynasty'.

It was shortly after this that Hudson confessed to a stunned world that he was not only gay but also dying of AIDS. This he did selflessly as a means of dispelling the malice and prejudice which AIDS sufferers have had to endure. In this brave attempt to create a better climate, Rock became a hero all over again, this time to a different audience.

In 1954 Rock proved himself a fully-fledged star when he appeared opposite Jane Wyman in the remake of *Magnificent Obsession*. It was at this time that the scummy tabloid magazine, *Confidential*, called Hudson's bosses to announce with pride that it had in its sweaty paw some damning evidence which proved beyond doubt that Rock was homosexual. With the arbitrary pragmatism so typical of Hollywood, they safeguarded Rock's secret by twisting the arm of the magazine and instead fed a minor gay actor to the lions. The scapegoat was George Nader.

With a career which only really required him to point his biceps at the camera and utter a few semi-intelligent words, Nader flaunted himself more on the covers of Hollywood fan magazines than he acted in films. Yet even his tiny successes in Hollywood were ruthlessly stamped out by the studio barons who now bought silence on Hudson for an exposé on Nader.

Nader made a last bid for the spotlight in the early 1960s with a couple of television series which failed, so instead he headed for West Germany where he became the number one star due to a succession of ersatz James Bond thrillers. But when spy films became passé, Nader brought his earnings back to Hollywood and retired in some degree of comfort.

The Hollywood publicists and gossip-columnists resorted to stop-gap tactics to protect Hudson. In 1955, he eloped with secretary Phyllis Gates and the result was a marriage which lasted three years. This created a smokescreen around his private life, as did his masculine achievement in *Giant* which was released the following year. For the next 15 years, chatterings about Rock's sexual preferences were dismissed as nothing more than malice or jealousy.

Hudson had, in fact, been fixed with a woman before this. The first girl he was seen flirting with in public, and thus by extension cavorting with in private, was the singer-dancer Vera-Ellen whose face may well be remembered for her role as Rosemary Clooney's sister in *White Christmas* (1954). Encouraged by Henry Willson, his agent-manager, with whom he was drinking at Ciro's nightclub in Hollywood in 1949, to go and talk to her, Rock interrupted her dance and the result was a series of highly public dates.

The Press Photographers' Costume Ball was not far off and Rock and Vera-Ellen stole the show by dressing up as 'Mr and Mrs Oscar', the Academy Award statuettes. Covered with gold paint, they sported splendid plastic heads, bathing costumes and swords from the props department. They won first prize. The gossip-writers claimed that Rock had proposed to the young lady but had been flatly rebuffed. And so the effective and reassuring publicity blanket gave the public not the slightest inkling that, not only would Rock never dream of marriage, but that he was also completely gay.

It was gay activist, Armistead Maupin, a columnist on the *San Francisco Chronicle*, who commented on this: 'Rock had learned the lesson well in Hollywood. He played by the rules. These rules say that you keep quiet about being gay and everyone will lie about it for you. The gossip columnists will make up girlfriends for you and everyone in Hollywood will know you're gay except the public.'

It was also to Maupin that Rock confessed he might finally reveal all to his public: 'Rock seemed to take to the idea and said, "One of these days I'm going to have a lot to tell." I thought it would be a good idea because he was actually the same in private life as on the screen: very masculine and natural. You could see the idea would be difficult for some men of his generation – he was never able to bring himself to go public about it.'

As the years passed, and Rock's PR machine was seen as nothing more than a desperate veil, stories about his real-life frolics hit the headlines. In the early 1970s, invitations to a party were sent out by a San Francisco gay couple who were known for their out-to-lunch gatherings. This time the event was to be the wedding reception of Rock Hudson and Jim Nabors. Hudson was able to dismiss such a practical joke with his virile charm but Nabors was kicked into touch by the powerful pen-pushers. Having signed to CBS in 1971 for his own variety show, he now found that it was cruelly cancelled. As in the case of George Nader the star had won out at the expense of the nonentity. Nabors upped and left Hollywood and settled in Hawaii. It was only through the loyalty of friends like Burt Reynolds, who cast Nabors in his films, that he was able to work again.

The sad irony in this case was that Hudson and Nabors were not in fact conducting an affair. Maupin, as usual, proves a credible source on the life of the star: 'Rock used to explain the story at dinner parties. In point of fact he and Nabors were just good friends. But the rumours made it impossible for them to be seen together, which is very sad.'

In the late 1970s and early 1980s one Tom Clark moved in with Rock Hudson. Because Rock had fired Henry Willson at the end of the 1960s, it was a simple convenience to refer to Clark as Rock's 'manager'.

The two had met when Clark was working as a publicist at MGM. He soon became the star's accounts adviser, secretary and friend and took part in plenty of Rock's well loved Hollywood pub crawls.

A confidante of Hudson's explains: 'It came to the point that he was dependent on Tom, because Tom babied him; he made sure Rock had a warm sweater on, he made his plane reservations, his dinner reservations, he made sure that Rock's clothes were out of the dry cleaners, he did everything for him. Rock loved that.'

Rock displayed a giant appetite for sex during his last 20 years in Hollywood. Famous and notorious men, not to mention would-be actors,

were able to share Rock's affections. One well known agent has said: 'Rock Hudson helped several people get started in show business.'

One in particular was a football player who lived with him in the early 1980s. Introduced by Rock to all the right people, he landed a plum role in

William Haynes, comic closet queen of the 1920s.

a national television series after which he cut Hudson dead and pretended never even to have met him, lest his own macho image be dented. He has since gone on to be the star of several national series.

It was this generosity which Rock possessed right to the end, when (and it must have been tough for him) he confessed his homosexuality for the benefit of others. By this time he had recorded 'Dynasty' on whose set he had arrived with sunken eyes and cheeks, as well as bony wrists and ankles. Desperate publicity claims about dieting and intentional weight-loss ('he loves the idea of being slender again') would not wash this time. But the old macho maverick died fittingly with the same respect he had enjoyed at the height of his career due to this last gesture of magnanimity.

At least Rock never suffered in the manner of other Hollywood homosexuals, many of whom were discarded by the studios. William Taten Tilden III, better known as Big Bill Tilden or 'Stumpfinger', was a star tennis player who soon became a silent movie actor. He had a predilection for young boys which finally nailed his career and shattered him personally. Once caught fondling a young boy in a car, he was later found waiting outside the school gates for another and finally used up all his money in the law courts. Abandoned by his high-flying friends, he died of a heart attack.

The likeable William Haines, a popular MGM star of the 1920s, went the same way. A comic queen who camped it up on set and would often greet male cast and crew with an affectionate pat on the bottom, he was finally caught with a sailor in a seedy downtown YMCA. His film career ended forthwith, although he went on to have a highly successful career as interior designer to the stars, becoming a millionaire in the process.

Hollywood homosexuals were always open to crude decisions by the dictators-on-high who would drop them at a snap if their leanings showed any sign of becoming public knowledge. In the context of cinema, what these actors really symbolize is the yawning gap between fantasy and reality. What the public believes is exactly what Hollywood wants it to.

Tortured Jimmy

Slick-back hair, macho posturing, adoring blonde floozies and fast cars do not normally suggest a man who is gay. Yet, since his death, James Dean has come to disappoint millions of female fans who worshipped his brooding behaviour and louche manner. At a time before the world would kiss the feet of Elvis, the earliest rock 'n' roll idol, Dean was the very first superhero to the first generation of teens. Like the marketing men behind every other teenage product since, Dean's studio bosses realized that here was the first generation to have a few spare cents in their pockets, so they sold Dean the image, Dean the style, and Dean the man who would leave the rest of manhood stranded as wimps.

And yet he was gay. A well established fact within the Hollywood community itself, it was also pointed out bluntly to Dean at a party in Malibu which he attended on the eve of his death. He had indulged in a bitter feud with an ex-lover, a man who noisily accused his chum of swanning around town with women for the sake of publicity. True though this certainly was, it has as much to do with Dean's tortured self as it has with the publicity machinations of Hollywood.

The teen idol jumped into his prized silver Porsche, notched it up to an unsafe 85 mph (137 km/h) at Chalome (near Paso Robles) and promptly sped headlong into an oncoming vehicle. He was found mangled. It was 30 September 1955, a date fixed in the minds of millions.

His hyperactive sex antics led to Dean's contracting VD and to his irritating habit of constantly scratching himself on the set of *Rebel Without A Cause* (1955). Natalie Wood, Nick Adams and Sal Mineo could only stare at their shoes in embarrassment but forgave him because they believed he was imitating his own hero, Marlon Brando. Brando has still to respond to this compliment.

Director Nicholas Ray was so offended by Dean's lewdness that he hauled him off to the chemist's for some soothing lotion.

Dean had developed an obsessive fancy for The Club, an East Hollywood bar for those of eccentric persuasion. Leather to the last, this welcoming void played host to Dean who spent most nights on the prowl. A newcomer to this intoxicating world, he became an immediate enthusiast of passion-by-punishment and took to the seedy milieu of boots and straps. His co-funsters at the venue soon began referring to him as the 'human ashtray', since, when stoned, he would crave for them to stub out their cigarette butts on his chest. After his death, the coroner made written mention of the 'constellation of keratoid scars' on Dean's body.

Some years before, Dean had skipped service in Korea by confessing his homosexuality. When asked by Hedda Hopper how he had avoided being dragooned into the army by the Fairmount Selective Service Unit, he replied wittily, 'I kissed the medic.'

Though no proof about Dean's first gay affair in Hollywood exists, he certainly moved in with Rogers Brackett shortly after his arrival in movieland. Brackett was older, a television director who lived on ritzy Sunset Plaza Drive and who treated Jimmy like a son. Close though they undoubtedly were, the fanzines spoke only of their father–son relationship.

Dean was a driven man, oscillating as he did between exhilaration and anxiety and so revealed all the primary symptoms of a typical manic depressive. Able to be vicious and charming in equal measure, he sulked his way through a short life as a tortured introspective, managing to offend almost everyone he met with his brooding arrogance. Yet it was the macho display of insecurity which seems the most powerful component in drawing fans towards him. *Rebel Without A Cause*, in particular, gave Dean the chance to parade his natural self-doubt and so give teenagers the world over a handy place to hang their growing pains.

His joyless soul was capable of relishing neither the success of *East of Eden* (1955) nor the guaranteed future of *Rebel Without A Cause* and *Giant* (1956), both of which had been completed but were still standing in line for release. Dean was to die first.

His childish petulance was well to the fore in his behaviour. Though he had only five months of acting experience, his status as a mollycoddled star led him to rudely insist on changes in both script and camera angles. He stamped his foot like the spoilt brat he was whenever a director dared to differ. Because he was a star, directors pretended to agree but in private they roasted him alive. Dean's insecurity was often on show as naked conceit and his infant pranks quickly became the talk of the town.

Probably thinking himself a rebel with a good cause, he enjoyed turning up at dinner jacket functions in T-shirt and jeans. Once at a gathering which included Karl Malden, Anthony Perkins and the revered Elia Kazan, the pouting oaf took his steak and flung it right out the window. Never heralded by his peers as a radical, he was instead scorned as a foolish prima donna. Spitting at the portraits of Bogart, Cagney and Muni which grace the hallowed reception area at Warners was a perfect match for his boorishness in restaurants where he generally asked for service by hammering the table or clattering the cutlery.

His addiction to dope also defined his behaviour. Commonly sleeping on friends' floors when he was too zonked to go home, he often forgot rehearsals as well as his lines. When he did manage to string a few words together, he often fluffed them and flounced off in a huff when reprimanded. The few journalists who succeeded in securing an interview with Dean came away talking about his habit of gushing non-sequiturs or sitting still like a mute, staring emptily at his questioner.

At first his death caused barely a ripple amongst his fans. It was Warners who wept loudest since Hollywood had never scored hits with movies by dead actors. Dean's death was to change this and usher in a wave of posthumous hero-worship which found its major groove in the world of rock 'n' roll: Jimi Hendrix, Janis Joplin, Jim Morrison, Elvis Presley and John Lennon were targets for the same rampant teenage addiction which was to startle Warners when they finally released *Rebel Without A Cause*. For once the studios did not contrive a hype but instead employed many extra hands to reply to the thousands of letters which flooded into the studio each day, many from fans who refused to believe that Dean was dead. Even Valentino never received this level of worship when he died.

Warners began to analyse the secret of Dean's success and soon realized that the tortured boy who was striving for manhood was a reflection of the lives of millions of fans who were cocking a snook at post-war austerity, sneering at their dour parents and insisting on having fun, fun, fun. Since Dean was not around to promote *Rebel*, Warners thoughtfully marketed Dean mementos, cards and models of his head to a greedy world. In a manner which was to be later duplicated by the sale of useless trivia which had belonged to John, Jimi, Janis and Elvis, bits of Jimmy's bike and part of his wrecked car were auctioned off at silly prices.

It is highly likely that Hollywood's most surprising gay would not have entered a movie studio after *Giant*, even if he had lived. Compulsively bound to a no-hope lifestyle of booze, drugs and kinky sex, he would have crumbled anyway. His gravestone in Fairmount, Indiana, is a symbol of his inarticulate nature which could never express his neurosis. It reads simply 'James Dean – 1931–1955'.

The most recent crop of Dean imitators (Richard Gere, Matt Dillon, Mickey Rourke) may have captured the style and swagger in slavish detail but they will never exude the troubled substance which was Jimmy's own.

Acknowledgements

The Publishers wish to thank the following organisations for their kind permission to reproduce the following photographs in this book:

Aquarius Picture Library 22–3, 35, 77, 81, 137;
The Kobal Collection 6, 11, 15, 47, 58, 63, 72, 93, 114–5, 121, 129, 143, 154;
National Film Archive 27;
Popperfoto 102–3.